Disclaimer:

In order to teach one must of necessity divulge. Some readers may be concerned that secrets belonging to the Capitular Degrees are set out in this course. To this concern I can only reply that there is nothing contained herein which has not already been stated in print by Thomas Smith Webb, Albert Mackey or any other author on the subject previously. I hold that, if one may find something in a book which bears an ISBN, and which therefore is in the public domain, it is no longer secret. I have drawn some information and images from websites, most of which are official Grand Chapter websites, and in one instance an anti-Masonic site which had a particularly good diagram!

Lastly, I can honestly claim that any errors in spelling, proofreading ort historical accuracy are my own, and I would welcome any constructive feedback, which you can send to the office of the Grand Secretary, found on page 6.

Piers A. Vaughan
January 2014

Revisions:

Without revising any of the contents, a review of the book revealed a number of mistyped words, which have been corrected in this version. No doubt, not all have been found!

M∴E∴ Piers A. Vaughan
August 2017

Table of Contents

Welcome to the Course

Welcome to the Royal Arch Development Course!

This Course is intended to make you more familiar with the history, background, ritual, symbols, teachings of the four Degrees which comprise the Capitular Degrees of the York – or American – Rite.

This course is intended to be taken after the Candidate has completed the Holy Royal Arch Degree, and preferably in a group setting, with an experienced Companion acting as Moderator for the group.

Those participating should previously have obtained:
- A copy of this course
- A copy of the ritual

It would also be most advantageous to have a copy of the Holy Bible at hand – hopefully the one with which you were presented during your Blue Lodge Degrees. While not essential – the course may be completed without one – it will vastly enhance your understanding and enjoyment of the lessons.

The relevant Degree and section of the course should have been read prior to the session.

Each session should take around one hour, and is intended to be run over three or four sessions (the Virtual Past Master and Fellowcraft sections can be run the same evening). The Companions present should be encouraged to read some sections of the text out loud (reading the whole text would take too long), and then the Moderator can ask the Questions in the quizzes of the Companions in turn. In answering the questions, the participants can reference the ritual and the course notes, as appropriate. It is hoped that the answers, and the Discussion Questions which follow, will provoke debate and an exchange of ideas in the group which will further help understanding.

Upon completion of the Course and payment of a nominal administration fee, all New York Chapter participants can receive a Certificate of Completion signed by the Grand High Priest, and a pin which may be worn at Royal Arch events.

You will note that the vast majority of the course focuses on the Holy Royal Arch Degree. This is to be expected. While the other Degrees contain element of great interest on the path, there is no doubt that the destination of the Capitular Degrees is the Royal Arch, which is also the completion of the Master Mason Degree and, in this series, the completion of the Masonic journey.

We hope you find the course interesting. If you have any comments or suggestions, we would be delighted to receive them. Please forward them to the Grand Secretary's Office, or by email to: grandram@aol.com.

Background and History of the Capitular Degrees

Early beginnings of the Capitular Degrees

While Symbolic Masonry manifested itself in the public domain in 1717 in the Goose and Gridiron Public House in London, it is clear that Lodges had existed for some time previously to that. This can be gleaned both from records and minutes (for example, the Minutes of certain Scottish Lodges, and the writings of Elias Ashmole), and from logical deduction that, in order to draw attention to their existence, the Lodges forming the first Grand Lodge must already have been in existence. And, since the first Lodges only sought to exercise jurisdiction over the Lodges in central London, by implication there must have been a number of Lodges elsewhere around England.

Figure 1- Elias Ashmole

This is an important fact, since, just as the origins of the Entered Apprentice and Fellowcraft Degrees cannot be determined with certainty (it is generally agreed among scholars that the Master Mason Degree was a later creation, appearing in the 1720s), the same is true for both the Mark and the Royal Arch Degrees. This means that versions of all three systems – Blue Lodge, Mark Lodge and Royal Arch Lodge or Chapter – were being practiced prior to 1717. The implications of this, assuming the Royal Arch Degree contained the lessons it currently does, are enormous. It means that the True Word was being given to certain Masons *before* a Degree conferring a Substitute Word was created.

This is important since, as respected Past General Grand High Priest William F. Kuhn states in his booklet *The Necessity of the Royal Arch to the Master Mason*, commenting on a letter he had received from Newton R. Parvin, Grand Secretary and Librarian of the Grand Lodge of Iowa, "This would tend to prove that before the legend of Hiram Abif was introduced into the Master's

Degree the True Word was communicated in the Master's Degree and not a substitute Word." So it is possible that the True Word ended up in the Royal Arch Degree, which was considered as important as the Third Degree, since it restored the True Word, and only ignorance and politics saw it ending up as a completely different Degree run by a different Grand Sovereign Body. One recent scholar described the lamentable fact that so many Master Masons never complete their understanding by going through the Royal Arch Degree as being like a person who reads the first several chapters of a book, then sets it aside without finishing it.

The Royal Arch was practiced both among the Moderns and the Antients. While the Degree was officially recognized as being part of the Antient Rituals, it was only barely tolerated among the Moderns, who did not consider it to be part of the official Degree system. This led to a number of conflicting applications of the law. For example, in 1766 the Grand Master, Lord Blayley supported the establishment of a Grand Chapter, whose primary role was to issue Charters, thereby 'regularizing Chapters, and even allowed it to meet at Great Queen Street. On the other hand, James Heseltine, Grand Secretary of UGLE from 1769 – 1780, wrote the following to the Province of Frankfurt-am-Main, which at the time was facing competition from the Rite of Strict Observance of Baron von Hund: "It is true that many of the Fraternity

Figure 2 - Lord Blayley

here belong to a Degree in Masonry say'd *to be superior* (italics mine) to the other three, call[ed] the Royal Arch. I have the honour to be a member of this Degree and its principles and proceedings are truly praiseworthy – but it is unknown in Grand Lodge, and all Emblems or Badges or distinction in that Degree are prohibited from being worn in GL."

A confusing situation indeed!

The Royal Arch was held in such esteem by the Antients, however, that it led Laurence Dermott, Grand Secretary of the Antients, to call the Royal Arch Degree the "very root, heart and marrow of Freemasonry."

In England, for example, at the Act of Union of 1813, which joined the Moderns and Antients into the United Grand Lodge of England & Wales (UGLE), the only Degrees which made it into the officially sanctioned list, according to the second Article of the Act of Union, were: "... that pure Antient Masonry consists of three degrees and no more, viz., those of Entered Apprentice, the Fellow Craft, and the Master Mason, including the Supreme Order of the Holy Royal Arch." An early attempt to reintroduce the Mark Master Degree was roundly defeated, and thereafter all the bodies we consider to be part of the York Rite are in England subject to completely independent Grand Bodies. However, it should be pointed out that while these Bodies are ignored by UGLE, many high ranking members of UGLE are enthusiastic members of them.

However, although the rituals of the Symbolic Degrees were established as part of the work of uniting the two Grand Lodges in England, the Royal Arch fared less well, and it was not until the 1840s that the first semi-official Ritual, the Sussex Ritual named in honor of the Duke of Sussex, was published. The early history of the Royal Arch in Europe can be found in many history books on the subject.

It is known that in most Scottish and Irish Lodges, many English ones, and from their Minutes most of the British colonies, that the Past Master, Mark and Royal Arch Degrees were habitually conferred in Symbolic Lodges. That there was a special – if honorary – Degree empowering a Master Mason to rule his Lodge as Worshipful Master, is without doubt. Originally it was probably as short as the one we practice today both in Lodge and Chapter, for the ceremony used in the United States is broadly the same. In England and elsewhere the Past Master Degree became increasingly elaborate, so that now it is considered the jewel in the crown of the English Masonic year, and the ceremony is indeed impressive and complex.

Figure 3 - The Duke of Sussex

One of the problems impacting the very survival of the Royal Arch Degree was the requirement that it could only be conferred upon those who had served as Worshipful Master of their Lodge. Given the relatively small number of Lodges compared to now, and the fact that not every Past Master availed himself of the opportunity – and indeed it may not even have been available in their District or Province – it was clear that the Royal Arch Degree, even if it was seen as the completion of the Masonic experience, could have failed before it took root. This was solved in the Act of Union by simply requiring a Candidate for the Royal Arch be a Master Masons of one year's standing (now reduced to one month). As an aside, while any Master Mason may become a Royal Arch Mason in England, one is however still required to have served as Master of a Lodge prior to being installed as one of the Three Principal Officers. In Scotland and Ireland there is a ceremony of Passing the Chair, similar to the Virtual Past Master, and in both countries a Candidate must receive the Mark and Past Master Degrees prior to being Exalted to the Royal Arch Degree.

In the meantime, the Royal Arch Degree was regularly practiced in the United States, and the Act of Union in England had no impact, since America had been independent from England for some thirty-seven years by then. Furthermore, it was part of a Degree *system* (the 'York' or 'American' Rite), whereas in England and most of Europe there were still many variations of the Royal Arch and other Degrees being worked both in Chapter and Lodges (for example, in Dermott's Book of

Constitutions, entitled *Ahiman Rezon* or Help to a Brother, published in 1756, we read the following comment in Rule II: "the Master of a particular Lodge has the right and authority of congregating the members of his own Lodge into a Chapter upon any emergency or occurrence.").

Figure 4 - Ahiman Rezon

While the requirement to receive the Past Master Degree was dropped at the Act of Union in England, it was considered too important a Landmark to be tampered with in the United States, and the Past Master Degree persists to this day.

But in the United States the Capitular Degrees have been unified since 1797, and the establishment of a standard series of Rituals, a progressive system of Degrees, together with an overarching American governing – later advisory – body with the authority to issue Charters to States and countries was almost entirely due to the work of one man, Thomas Smith Webb, whose diligence and commitment make him a key figure in the history of American Freemasonry.

Codification of the Degrees in the United States – the "York" or "American" Rite

The 'York' Rite is a name only used in the United States, since it is only here that a number of different Degrees were collected together into a progressive system. Indeed, the source of the term 'York Rite' is somewhat dubious, since it is based upon an unprovable legend, fondly held by Freemasons in the 18th Century, that English Masonry originated in York, either under King Edwin of Northumbria who converted to Christianity in 627 CE and ordered the York Masons to build a cathedral; or King Athelstan in 926 CE. Athelstan either organized or reorganized the Masons in York at that time, gave them a Charter, and placed his son Edwin in charge of them. Incidentally the Antients claimed this ancestry on their Warrants; and the Moderns claimed that same authority was "transferred many years ago to London. Ours is the real Ancient Grand Lodge of York"!

While this is certainly a glamorous story, there is no actual proof that the Charter issued by Athelstan bears a direct and unbroken lineage to our present Lodges, and indeed this is only one of many theories about our origins, and sits alongside the Knights Templar, the Ancient Egyptians, the Mediterranean Mystery Schools, and the Rosicrucians to name but a few of the more popular ones.

Figure 5 - King Athelstan

However, the name 'York Rite' to describe the system of Degrees in the United States, and to distinguish itself from the 'Scottish Rite', which are a series of 33 Degrees which originated in France, has become established, and is in common use today. Incidentally the reason that system is called the 'Scottish Rite' is because of its association with the Scottish monarchy who, beginning with James II of England, was exiled to France after attempting to reestablish Roman Catholicism in England, and he and his successors, Pretenders to the English throne, signed Masonic Charters. Sometimes the 'York' Rite is more correctly referred to as the 'American Rite', since it was created in the United Stated. Both 'York Rite' and 'American Rite' will be used interchangeably here.

In the United States, the first record of a version of the Royal Arch Degree being worked is at Fredericksburg Lodge, VA in 1753, the Lodge in which George Washington was Initiated, Passed and Raised. Despite many attempts, to date no credible record of Washington receiving the Royal Arch Degree has been found[1]. At that time the Royal Arch Degree (like the Mark Degree) was conferred in Lodges as well as Chapters – as indeed they were in England, Scotland and Ireland – and it was not until the system was codified in the 1790 that Chapters alone conferred the Degree. In 1758 the Antients Grand Lodge issued a Charter to a lodge in Pennsylvania, and they can be assumed to have exercised the rights and privileges of an Antient Lodge, which included conferring the Past Master and Royal Arch Degrees. Unfortunately, there are few records which survive from this period, and it is also quite certain that during the Revolutionary War, many Lodges suspended

---

[1] Interestingly, however, Washington Lodge possesses a portrait of George Washington in a white apron bordered with red; and his possessions included a number of Royal Arch artifacts. Not proof positive, but a hint, perhaps.

activities or relocated to avoid the worst of the fighting. This can be seen, for example, in the history of Freemasonry in New York State, where all the Lodges in Manhattan, with the exception of St. John's Lodge No. 1, A.Y.M., went dormant or relocated outside New York City during this time. It is to be expected that, given the pressure of the War of Independence on the ability of Symbolic Lodges to meet, the Mark and Royal Arch Degrees were rarely worked during this time.

In the 1780s a number of Chapters came into existence, some styling themselves Grand Chapters in order to issue Charters to others. For example, *Old Royal Arch Chapter* wrote to the Grand Lodge of New York in 1783 requesting the Grand Master and Grand Officers preside over their affairs. Upon the establishment of a Grand Chapter in New York State on March 14, 1798, some of the older Chapters refrained from joining the new Grand Body. However, in 1806 *Old Chapter* and *Washington Chapter*, both based in New York City, joined and were accorded the honor of being No. 1 and No. 2 respectively (*Old Chapter* was later renamed *Ancient Chapter No. 1*).

By now several Grand Chapters existed, in New York, Pennsylvania and Maryland. In Boston, the issue of obtaining a sovereign Warrant was discussed, showing that the idea of making Capitular Masonry independent from Symbolic Masonry was a major topic at that time. This led to discussions on the establishment of a ruling body, and on September 11, 1797, St. Andrew's Chapter in Boston approved a motion that "the High Priest be requested to write Br. Webb on the subject of a union of the chapters". In October, Thomas Smith Webb and John Hanmer of Temple Chapter in Albany visited Boston. Having recently published the *Freemason's Monitor or Illustrations of Masonry*, Webb's Masonic reputation was immense, and he had both the vision and stamina to see such a project through to fruition. Following the conferral of a number of Degrees, on October 24, 1797, representatives from St. Andrew and Cyrus Chapters met with Webb and Hanmer to

Figure 6 - Thomas Smith Webb

discuss establishing a General Grand Chapter. Companion Webb presided, and a letter was sent to other Chapters inviting them to attend a Grand Convocation at Hartford, Connecticut.

Figure 7 - Ephraim Kirby

On January 24, 1798 delegates from nine Chapters met in Hartford, and on January 26 a Constitution was approved which declared sovereign jurisdiction over Massachusetts, Connecticut, Rhode Island, New Hampshire, Vermont and New York. Under the Constitution, this General Grand Chapter assumed control of the Mark Master, Past Master, Most Excellent Master and Royal Arch Degrees. Ephraim Kirby was elected first General Grand High Priest, an honor which surely should have gone to Thomas Smith Webb. It is a testament to the integrity of the man that he stepped aside to ensure that Connecticut would become part of the alliance. By 1802 Thomas Smith Webb Had published a reprint of his *Monitor*, which now contained comments on the Capitular and Templar Degrees, and South Carolina, Kentucky and Ohio had by now joined the General Grand Chapter.

The 'York' or 'American' Rite Degrees were then, as now, as follows:

Symbolic (Blue) Lodge
1. Entered Apprentice
2. Fellowcraft
3. Master Mason

Chapter of Royal Arch Masons
4. Mark Master
5. Past Master
6. Most Excellent Master
7. Royal Arch Mason

Council of Cryptic Masons
8. Royal Master
9. Select Master
10. Super Excellent Master

Commandery of Knights Templar
8. Order of the Red Cross
9. Order of Malta
10. Order of the Temple

A few points are worth noting. While the Royal Arch Degrees are open to any Master Mason, any Mason wishing to join a Cryptic Council must be a Royal Arch Companion. In New York the

Cryptic Degrees are optional, which means a Royal Arch Masons can petition to join a Commandery of Knights Templar directly (which is why the three Orders have been numbered 8., 9., and 10. above). In a number of States the Cryptic Degrees are a prerequisite to joining the Order of the Temple. In all cases the Super Excellent Master Degree (10. In the Cryptic Rite series) is an optional Degree, and possession of the Royal and Select Master Degrees are sufficient to progress to the Templar Orders.

Note also that, while the Chapter and Cryptic Degrees are open to any Master Mason, the Order of the Temple requires a Statement of Adherence to the Christian Religion, and the Orders of Malta and the Temple take much of their symbolism from the New Testament, with many direct quotations from the Scriptures.

The colors associated with the four York Rite Bodies (for the Symbolic Lodge is seen as being part of the 'York' Rite) are Blue for the Symbolic Lodge, Red for the Chapter, Purple for the Council and White (and Black) for the Commandery. The fact that these are also the colors of the Royal Arch banners and veils – and for that matter the first four banners of the Order of Malta – is no coincidence.

But perhaps the most important point of all is the fact that these Degrees form a coherent path for the serious student of our Gentle Craft. Regardless of whether one continues through the Capitular and Chivalric Degrees, every country recognizes that the Royal Arch Degree as the completion of the Master Mason Degree, and without having experienced this rich Ritual which confers the True Word upon its Companions, that which had been lost until the wisdom of future generations brought it to light, one has not experienced the full story of Freemasonry as it was intended from the year it first came to the attention of the general public.

General Grand Chapter and the Structure of Capitular Freemasonry

The General Grand Chapter has no direct authority over its constituent Grand Chapters (unlike Masonic Templary, where the Grand Encampment is sovereign). It does however, exercise sovereignty over a number of individual Chapters around the world; and when a new Grand Chapter is chartered, relinquishes authority in that jurisdiction to the new Grand Chapter.

In its earliest days, the General Grand Chapter was indeed sovereign, and originally each State had a Deputy Grand High Priest. However, this was changed and in 1859 a resolution was passed to revise the wording of the Constitution to state that the powers of the General Grand Chapter were derived from the State Bodies, and that they enjoyed sovereign jurisdiction over their territories.

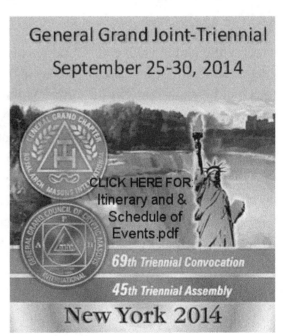

Figure 8 - 69th Triennial of General Grand Chapter

By 2014, General Grand Chapter comprised forty-seven States, several Canadian Provinces, and a number of countries in Central and Latin America, Europe, Asia and Africa; including Quebec, British Columbia, Romania and Brazil to name but a few.

The permanent Members of General Grand Chapter are the Past Grand High Priests of affiliated Grand Chapters, along with the elected General Grand Chapter Officers. This, including the Elected Members of State Grand Chapters, forms the voting body, which meets every three years in a Triennial. The elected Officers of the General Grand Chapter are: General Grand High Priest, General Grand King, General Grand Scribe, General Grand Treasurer and General Grand Secretary; as well as the

Figure 9 - Ritual Excellence Jewel awarded by GGC

Past General Grand High Priest in an advisory and *ex-officio* capacity. The General Grand High Priest appoints ten Deputy General Grand High Priests, seven of which look after the regions of the United States, and three the overseas territories. Each territory also appoints an Ambassador, who is a Past Grand High Priest, to represent the General Grand Chapter in that State.

The General Grand Chapter supervises the growth of Chapters in new territories, until they are in a position to petition for a Warrant as an independent Grand Chapter. It issues Warrants, and provides a clearing house for ideas, particularly at the Triennial. In addition it is responsible for education and research, particularly through its quarterly magazine, the Royal Arch Mason.

It also makes available a number of awards, including one for Ritual excellence, Bronze, Silver and Gold distinguished service medals, and membership incentive programs. It also supports several charities which focus on auditory deficiencies under the umbrella of Royal Arch Research Assistance (or RARA), and maintains the George Washington Memorial Royal Arch Room in Alexandria, VA.

At a state level Chapters are organized much like Blue Lodges. There is a Grand Chapter presided over by the Grand High Priest (and occasionally also a Deputy Grand High Priest), who is the executive head of Royal Arch Masonry in in that State, and who is assisted by the elected officers, the Grand King, Grand Scribe, Grand Treasurer and Grand Secretary, and a number of appointed Grand Line Officers, including Grand Representatives. At a local level Chapters are organized into Districts, each supervised by a District Deputy Grand High Priest, who is assisted by an Assistant Grand Lecturer. Once a year a Grand Convocation is held, presided over by the Grand High Priest, at which business is conducted, Grand Line Officers elected and installed, and which is attended by sitting High Priests, Kings and Scribes, as well as visitors from a number of other States. The Chapters are warranted by the Grand Chapter, with authority to confer the four Capitular Degrees, under the leadership of the High Priest, assisted by the other members of the High Council, the King and Scribe.

New York's Unique Place in History

Any member of the Grand Chapter of New York, may be justly proud of his heritage. Along with the long and impressive history of Grand Chapter and the larger than life characters associated with it, consider those giants of Freemasonry who worked to establish the York Rite as one of the largest Masonic Bodies in the world, and those men who led it through its earliest days.

Thomas Smith Webb single-handedly established both the General Grand Chapter and the Grand Encampment of Knights Templar, and DeWitt Clinton, Governor of New York State, largely responsible for the construction of the Erie Canal served as General Grand High Priest.

It is a particular honor that, at the time of writing this course in 2013, M∴E∴ Edmund Dale Harrison, a New York Mason, is General Grand High Priest of the General Grand Chapter, which has seen significant international expansion under his leadership; while Sir Knight David Dixon Goodwin, another New York Mason, is Grand Master of the Grand Encampment of Knights Templar, and September 2014 saw the celebration of 69th Triennial of General Grand Chapter in Buffalo, where DeWitt Clinton performed the first ceremony of the Wedding of the Waters, to celebrate a continuous navigable waterway between the Atlantic Ocean at New York City to the Great Lakes at Buffalo.

Overview of the Capitular Degrees

In the York Rite, the four Capitular or 'Red' Degrees (as opposed to the 'Blue' Degrees of Lodge) continue immediately after the first three Masonic Degrees, continuing the Entered Apprentice, Fellowcraft and Master Mason Degree. The next four which comprise the Capitular Degrees are:

4. The Honorary Degree of Mark Master Mason
5. The Virtual Past Master Degree
6. The Most Excellent Master Degree
7. The Holy Royal Arch Degree

The first three Degrees take place in a Lodge, but the Royal Arch Degree is held in a Chapter. Since all four Degrees are governed by a Charter issued by the Grand Chapter of the State, all meetings Open and Close on the Royal Arch Degree, which is the equivalent of Opening a Lodge on the Third Degree. It is on the Royal Arch Degree that all business is transaction, votes taken and minutes read and approved. The Chapter is lowered to the appropriate Degree to confer the Mark Master, Virtual Past Master and Most Excellent Master Degrees.

Figure 10 - The Rejected Stone

The **Degree of Mark Master Mason** is called a Honorary Degree primarily because, in the York Rite, it is considered an intermediate Degree on the way to receiving the Royal Arch Degree; whereas in many other jurisdictions, for example England, it is a separate Rite chartered by a Sovereign Body, in whose Lodges members meet several times a year, business is transacted on the Mark Degree, the Officers' line is progressive, and there are annual Elections and a unique Installation ritual for the Right Worshipful Master who presides.

The Degree of Mark Master is nowadays a combination of two former Degrees – Mark Man (equivalent in level to the Fellowcraft Degree) and Mark Master. The Degree contains many important teachings, and bases its legend upon the tradition of operative Masons who engraved their work with a personal sign or 'mark', by which their work was identified.

The **Degree of Virtual Past Master** is a reminder that there was once a time when the Royal Arch Degree was either considered a part of the Master Masons Degree, or a Degree which could only be conferred upon those who had presided as Master of a regular Lodge. This had proved extremely limiting in terms of numbers eligible to join, and to open up the beautiful Royal Arch Degree (and to ensure its survival!), a Degree of *Passing The Chair* was created, by which Master Masons could sit in the East and receive the Past Master's grip and word, and be thereby eligible to receive

Figure 11 - Past Master's Jewel

the Royal Arch Degree. While many countries have replaced this requirement with a simpler one that Candidates only be Master Masons for a period of time prior to receiving it, this quaint relic of former times has been preserved in the York Rite as a precursor to receiving the Royal Arch Degree.

Figure 12 - Keystone being placed

The Degree also contains the word 'virtual', to emphasize the fact that, although the Brother has received the Word and Grip of Past Master, this is only as a prerequisite to his receiving the Royal Arch Degree, and in no way qualifies him to govern a regular Blue Lodge. It is quite possible – and not uncommon – for a Mason to be a Royal Arch Mason and a Virtual Past Master prior to being installed in the East in his Lodge and receiving the 'Secrets of the Chair' in that context.

It has been suggested by some scholars that the **Degree of Most Excellent Master** was originally part of a more elaborate ending to the Mark Degree, since it deals with the placing of the Keystone which plays such a central part in that Degree. Nowadays it is an independent Degree whose subject is the completion of the Temple, and contains the unique Masonic action of removing one's apron within the open Lodge room.

Finally, the **Degree of Holy Royal Arch** is the pinnacle of the Capitular System. In this complex and beautiful Degree, the Candidate is Exalted to become a Royal Arch Mason and becomes a Companion. He continues to be a Brother, of course, but the term Companion reminds

Figure 13 - English Royal Arch Jewel

him that he is now considered to be in a closer relationship with his fellow travelers. Of course, the singularly most important thing about this Degree is that he receives the True Word of a Master Mason.

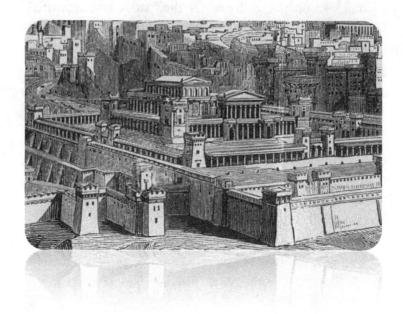

Figure 14 - King Solomon's Temple

The Placing of the Degrees in the Ritual Timeline

The time periods covered by the Capitular Degrees largely follow those of the Blue Lodge Degrees. However, due to its dual nature, the first part of the Mark Degree actually takes place while the Candidate is still a Fellowcraft, which is indicated by the manner in which he wears his apron. In second part of the Degree he is once again clothed as a Master Mason, and the action takes place shortly after the death of Grand Master Hiram Abif.

The Virtual Past Master Degree follows, and reflects the Installation of a Master of a Lodge, which it is meant to emulate, although in a shortened manner. Remember the word and grip received as an Installed Master are not intended to replace the Substitute Grip and Word of Master Mason. It is a separate ceremony in itself which empowers the Master to rule his Lodge. In the United States the act of conferring the Master's Grip and Word upon a well-qualified Candidate for the Chair of King Solomon is called an Investiture, to emphasize the fact that it is not a new Degree in or of itself. However, the Degree of Virtual Past Master reflects the origins of the Degree, which in other countries, itself developed into an elaborate ceremony considered the equivalent of receiving another Degree, since it is sometimes conferred in a Board of Past Masters, with its own ceremonies, legend, obligations, several signs and the grip. And following this the regular members of the Lodge are readmitted, being informed that 'during your temporary absence, the Brother has been duly entrusted with the Secrets of the Chair and Installed as Master of his Lodge.'

The Most Excellent Master Degree celebrates the completion of the Temple, with Solomon, King of Israel and Hiram King of Tyre receiving the Brethren into the Degree, while fondly remembering their fallen friend, Grand Master Hiram Abif.

The Royal Arch Degree is set some four hundred years following the completion of the Temple. Much time has indeed passed, and many Kings have sat upon the throne of Israel. Over that time the Israelites offended God by turning to worship other Gods, and this culminated with the overthrow of Israel and the destruction of the Temple by Nebuchadnezzar, King of Persia, when most of the Jews were scattered abroad and a large number led into captivity in Babylon. Seventy years later, under the leadership of a Prince of the House of Israel, Zerubbabel, a group of descendants return to Jerusalem to rebuild the Temple. The Royal Arch Degree takes place during an early time in this activity of rebuilding

Mark Master Mason Degree

Origins of the Degree

It has long been known that, throughout the history of stone buildings, Stonemasons have identified their work with a peculiar mark which they engraved on their work. It is also believed that these may be familial marks, passed from father to son. Whether these were placed as a mark of pride, or as a method for being paid for their work is not definitively known. What we do know is that these marks were never intended to be seen, as we shall see later.

The earliest mention of marks as part of a ritual are to be found in Operative documents originating in Scotland, including the Schaw Statutes of 1598 and Kilwinning Lodge in 1698, among others.

Figure 15 - The Schaw Statutes

However, the first mention of marks in Speculative Freemasonry appear after 1717, although most scholars agree a form of the Degree was worked much earlier than this. However, it would appear that such Degrees were not at all standardized, and probably grew up and developed in local pockets. The earliest record of Mark Masonry as a true, speculative body is on September 1, 1769 in the minutes of the Chapter of Friendship of Portsmouth, England, which mention that Thomas Dunckerley, Pro Grand Master, made a number of those present Mark Masons and Mark Masters, each choosing their mark. Interestingly enough it mentions that one Brother present was 'Thomas Webb'! Thomas Smith Webb was instrumental in establishing the York Rite Bodies in the United States – but there is no evidence whatsoever that *our* Thomas Smith Webb ever traveled to England. The earliest known Scottish record is dated

October 8, 1770; and in Ireland August 27, 1775, granted by the 'Knight Templars of Kinsale, County Cork.'

In England, after the Act of Union in 1813, Section 1 of the revised Constitutions stated that the only Degrees recognized by the United Grand Lodge of England (UGLE) were "…those of the Entered Apprentice, the Fellow Craft, and the Master Mason including the Supreme Order of the Holy Royal Arch." Since many Lodges had been practicing a progressive series which closely paralleled the York Rite (and our own system) in which it was a requirement for the Mark Degree to be conferred prior to receiving the Royal Arch Degree, this was now no longer necessary in England. However, it is interesting to note that in many of the British colonies, including Australia, India and South Africa, the Mark Degree was still conferred as a prerequisite; and even in England the Mark Degree, instead of fading into oblivion, gathered under the Grand Mark Lodge in 1856, which immediately started to issue Charters for Mark Lodges, with the blessing – or at least indifference – of UGLE.

Figure 16 - St. Bartholomew's Church, Brighton, UK

Incidentally, the Royal Ark Mariner Degree, which is considered to be one of the oldest rituals, is 'moored' to a Mark Lodge in many countries, and conferred within that Lodge. Both Degrees embody old Masonic traditions: the telling of the story of King Solomon's Temple and of Noah's Ark. Both prominently feature a celestial arc: one as if made of water in the airy heavens; and one made of stone (or earth) soaring above the heads of those in the Temple. One possible reason for this is the fact that many of the early Guilds put on Miracle Plays in medieval times; and while each craft might have its Patron Saint, they would also delight in enacting Biblical stories of special significance to their trade. Stonemasons would naturally gravitate towards the telling of the building of the Tower of Babel, or King Solomon's Temple; while the Woodcutters would very likely have been inspired by the tale of Noah's Ark, with its wooden boat of literally biblical proportions. This fascination has continued until more recent times, as we see both in the obsessive searches for the remains of Noah's Ark in Turkey, and even in the proportions of St. Bartholomew's Church in Brighton, England, built in the 1870s by Fr. Arthur Wagner to the exact biblical measurement of the Ark.

The Mark Degree in the United States

In the United States, early versions of the Mark Degree were brought across from England, and particularly Ireland by the military, and it is clear that there would have been a number of versions in existence around the colonies. Some of the Lodges also followed English tradition: for example, St. John's Lodge No. 1, A.Y.M., New York possessed a Charter from the Premier Grand Lodge (now sadly lost) which purportedly gave them the authority to confer the Mark Degree in addition to the Blue Lodge Degrees. This was not uncommon prior to the Act of Union. Similarly, Independent Royal Arch Lodge No. 2 make a strong claim to be allowed to confer the Royal Arch Degree, saying records demonstrate this permission dates back to the mid-1700s. However, two events served to unify and freeze the Mark Degree once and for all.

The first was a series of meetings or conventions held by a small number of early Chapters between 1796 and 1797, from which, on October 24, 1797 in Boston, the General Grand Chapter was created. In January 1798, the General Grand Chapter of the Northern United States was formally established. This body, while advisory, chartered Grand Chapters and provided guidance across the United States, and more recently across the world.

The second was the creation of a Freemason's Monitor in 1797, by Thomas Smith Webb. This compilation of Rituals included the Mark Master, Past Master, Most Excellent Master and Royal Arch Mason Degrees. At the time, there was already considerable standardization of ritual between the several States conferring them, so Webb did not *invent* the rituals we now use. However, he considerably expanded the Most Excellent Master Degree, introduced poems and music into the rituals (he was an accomplished musician and conductor) and most importantly, his printing of the Monitor helped solidify the rituals into an unchanging body of work. Although the body of Degrees as a whole is still commonly referred to as the 'York Rite', it would be more proper to call them the 'American Rite', for the versions we have used in the United States for over two hundred years were finalized here, in the former British colonies.

The Rule of Three

As we see in the Blue Lodge Degrees, the number three features prominently in this Degree. There are three Overseers, three Rulers of the Craft, the Candidate enters with two other Craftsmen carrying three stones for inspection. Once more this number reflects the Sacred Delta of Divinity, and implies that all work is performed under His sleepless eye. In some versions of the Mark Degree He is referred to as the Great Overseer.

Figure 17 - Sacred Delta.

The Overseers

The three key additional Officers in a Mark Lodge are the Junior, Senior and Master Overseers placed, according to the ritual, at the South Gate, West Gate and East Gate respectively. Effectively this means they double the positions of the Junior Warden, Senior Warden and Worshipful Master. Originally, they did not exist and their functions were taken by the JW, SW and WM instead. However, over time they were included in rituals as an important representation of those Masons responsible for supervising the work – a theme which becomes increasingly important through the Capitular Degrees.

"Good Work, True Work, Square Work"

One of the interesting sections of the Mark Degree centers upon the presentation of three Ashlars for inspection. Two are accepted because they are 'good work, true work, square work.' In other words, those stones tested – and therefore presumably carved – using only a square as a guide are accepted. However, the design of the third stone requires both a square and compasses to create: the top is an arc and the mark is contained within a circle. This is a new Order of Masonry. Initially the stone designed by square and compasses is rejected, but later it is relocated and given a position of prominence in the building.

This indicates an important transition which takes place between the Blue and the Capitular Degrees. While the Square was sufficient to design the stones or ashlars required for general building in the Entered

Figure 18 - George Washington placing the cornerstone of the Capitol

Apprentice, Fellowcraft and Master Mason Degrees, those of the Capitular Degrees now employ the compasses as well. The stone is recognized in the Mark Degree, positioned at the head of the Principal Arch in the Most Excellent Master Degree, and is one of the discoveries which ultimately leads to the recovery of the Master's Word in the Royal Arch Degree.

The Mark

In early times, the Masons carving a stone would place an identifying mark upon it. This was so the inspectors of the work could identify the craftsman responsible for each component stone. As a sign of approval, they often added their mark to the stone, to show that it had passed inspection and was ready to be employed in construction. A third mark was often added, to indicate which place in the building the stone was to be used. Nowadays we can see evidence of such marks on stones in castles, cathedrals and other buildings. However, it was never intended that these marks would be seen. Immediately after the walls were erected they would normally be covered in mortar or plaster and therefore remain invisible, unless the plaster fell off at a later period. Operative Masons' marks would be recorded in a Book of Marks, and marks would often be handed down within a family.

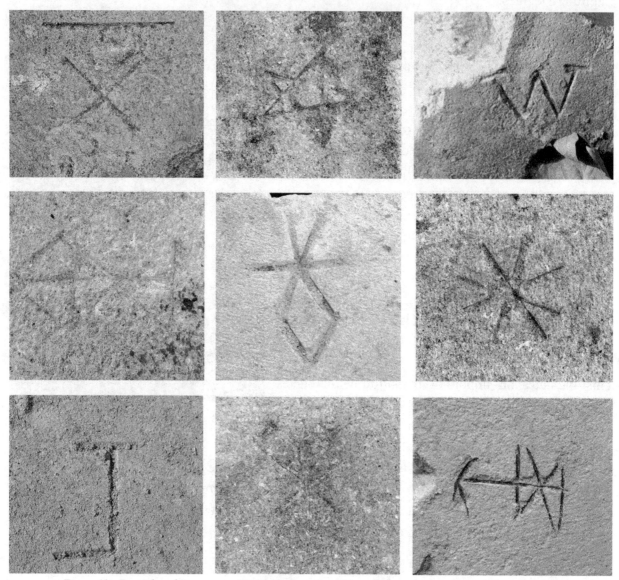

Figure 19 - Examples of Stonemason Marks ([source: http://blog.underoverarch.co.nz/tag/masons-marks/]

In the ceremony, the Candidate admits the mark on the stone is not his own. Until he has had his work approved he is not entitled to a mark and therefore to collect wages. Later in the ceremony he is presented with a sheet of paper and told to select and draw his mark, which will then be recorded in the Book of Marks of the Lodge. In some other countries, he is either given his mark, or offered a choice between two, but here he draws his own. While some early marks were quite elaborate, nowadays the Candidate is normally advised to select a simple design made up of straight lines. This task must be completed and his design handed in to the Secretary before he can receive the Royal Arch Degree.

Figure 20 - Example of the Hindu 'bindi' or red dot representing the Third Eye or pineal gland

However, we should remember that the word 'mark' has more than one meaning in the English language. As well as meaning a physical sign placed upon an object to denote authorship, it can also denote ownership, for example as in the branding of an animal, or in Biblical times, slaves. Again, it can denote a setting apart for religious or other purposes, such as the red dot placed over the 'third eye' by many Hindus, and the elaborate body paint used in tribes from the early Celts to Native American tribes. In the Bible, we are also reminded that a mark can be a divine sign of separation as well. We have already noted this in the story of Moses, where the Children of Israel marked their doorposts with

blood to identify themselves as Children of 'I AM', to avoid the death of their firstborn sons. In the case of Cain, it was a mark of shame, but which also preserved his life (Genesis 4:15, "And the Lord set a mark upon Cain, lest any finding him should kill him"). Again, in Ezekiel we read that God tells the man clothed with linen to "Go through the midst of the city, through the midst of Jerusalem, and set a mark upon the foreheads of the men that sigh and that cry for all the abominations that be done in the midst thereof" (Ezekiel 9:4).

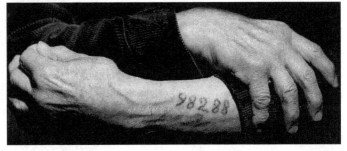

Figure 21 - The horror of branding a person set aside for persecution

Figure 22 - Self Made Man by Robbie Carlyle

So, the idea of a mark has a number of significations. Whilst it is used by man at a mundane level to identify his creations (carved stones) and property (cows, sheep), it is also used as a means by which God identifies His own people. Man may be tasked with shaping himself into a Spiritual Stone, fit to be used in the Temple not made with hands; but God is not absent in the process. He is, after all, the Grand Architect, and all that we do is in conformity with His Will. We may provide the labor, but it is He who provides the blueprint. Remember God says: "…and (I) will give him a white stone, and in the stone a new name written, which no man knoweth saving he that receiveth it." (Rev. 2:17). Like the mark covered with mortar in an old cathedral, we receive the name known only to us and God, which he will use to identify us when He calls us home.

Rejection of the Stone

The Junior and Senior Overseer pass the stone, but the Master Overseer calls a council of Overseers, and they collectively decide to reject the stone as neither being oblong nor square, nor having the mark of any of the workmen upon it. It appears the Overseers are neither familiar with stones which are not square, nor with the mark of Hiram Abif, since the keystone bears his name. The reason is revealed later in the ceremony, when King Solomon explains that this work was assigned to Grand Master Hiram Abif himself, and since he is usually responsible for the Designs, it is not until some Craftsmen look at the Trestleboard themselves that they see the 'Peculiar Stone' and Hiram's mark.

They heave the stone over among the rubbish. The act of 'heaving the stone over' suggest it as thrown over a wall. In early days, there is a tradition that if a workman offered up a faulty piece of work it was the workman who was heaved over the wall where he presumably fell to his death! In the Middle Ages, the stone was carried away on a bier, as though dead. If we are taught to be Living Stones in our ritual, the lesson of being discarded if found unworthy should be particularly significant to us. However, in this case the lesson that the stone is in fact the most important in the edifice, and yet is

Figure 23 - Two curiously familiar stones in front of the door of St. Polycarp in Lyons, France

discarded by those not recognizing its true worth is of particular importance.

"An Imposter!"

Figure 24 - A half shekel used as Temple tax

Following this, the Fellowcraft depart to receive their wages. Interestingly, while we are told in the Blue Lodge that Entered Apprentices earned no wages, but received food, clothing and lodging while they trained, Fellowcraft received corn, wine and oil as wages. Now we see how the Mark Master Mason is paid in *specie*, a penny a day, received on the sixth hour of the sixth day of the week, or Friday before the Sabbath. Traditionally, in ancient times the Jews would divide the daylight hours into twelve equal periods, which means an hour was not necessarily sixty minutes. So, the implication is, that work ceased around the middle of the daylight period, giving the workmen time to gather up their belongings, collect their wages, and be home before sundown.

In the Degree, the Brethren assemble to receive their wages twice, and on each occasion a different important lesson is taught. In the Mark Degree, we receive an explanation of something said by the Senior Warden of his duties in Blue Lodge: "…to pay the Craft their wages if any be due." Now we see him practice that duty, by repairing to his apartment (this simply means a room in the Temple) to pay the Craft their wages, which as we have learned, was one penny a day, or presumably six pennies a week. Remember this is all symbolic!

The Craftsmen thrust their hand through an opening to receive them, with their fourth and fifth fingers curled over a picture of their mark. This mark was compared to those in the Book of Marks, and if it was listed the coin was placed between their index and third fingers, which they then withdrew from the opening. In some older Lodges, you can find a circular opening covered by a panel in the Inner Door. However, it is more customary to have a wicket, which is a custom box, or a vertical panel of latticework with a circular or triangular hold cut into it, so the Brethren can see the action.

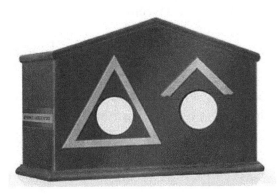

Figure 25 - Mark Degree Wicket used by the Senior Warden in English Mark Lodges

Figure 26 - Beware the left hand…

This first time the Candidate is not carrying a mark, so when he thrusts his hand through the opening it is seized and he is threatened with the loss of his right hand, a terrible penalty for a man making his living through the use of his hands. Remember, he is not just losing his livelihood: even in the Arabic cultures nowadays the left hand is seen as inferior and used for the more unclean roles such as cleaning oneself in the bathroom. He will now have to perform all his activities – including eating, and greeting colleagues – with his 'unclean' hand.

The Challenge

The Candidate is conducted to the Right Worshipful Master (in some rituals, the Senior Deacon drags the Candidate by his right ear), who challenges the Candidate, firstly by asking for someone to vouch for him, and then to prove himself a Fellowcraft by the grip and password. Since the

Candidate is clearly not yet a Mark Master he neither has the correct grip nor the password. Requiring a Brother to vouch for him recalls an earlier version of the ritual, still practiced in Ancient Chapter No. 1, New York, when the Conductor of the now blindfolded Candidate is asked: "Has he made suitable proficiency in the preceding Degrees to entitle him to this, and is he vouched for?" The Conductor replies: "He has, and I vouch for him."

He is told to return to the Quarries and this time to return with a suitable specimen of his work to pass the Overseers' tests and to entitle him to receive the correct grips, signs and words to entitle him to receive wages. This he does, his work, being 'an oblong or a square', is accepted, and he is given permission to proceed in the Degree. And yet the fact that he never claimed the work to be his own is never considered. His crime, it appears, was to reach for something which it is not yet his right to aspire to: he must prove himself proficient in his existing duties before being granted access to higher wisdom.

Given that the Degree has a pass grip and word, and a real grip and word, it would be logical to expect the pass grip and word to be given here, as a reward for his work, and that he would give these to the Deacon in order to be admitted to the next part of the Degree. This is how all pass grips and words work in Blue Lodges in other countries. Strangely, however, the pass grip and word are given in the next section, immediately prior to the real grip and word. This is probably something which became confused at an early time in the ritual's history, and has never been rectified.

Transition to Master Mason

All the preceding work has been a preamble to the actual Degree itself. Indeed, the Mark Degree is unusual in that it contains both a prologue and an epilogue. Prior to the Degree itself we have the scenes where the Candidate presents work not his own, is chastised for this, then returns with work accepted as his. Following the Degree, during the Lodge Closing, we have the further scene in which the Workmen discuss their wages, and the Right Worshipful Master issues his challenge to them.

At this point it is assumed that a passage of time has taken place. The Fellowcraft has proven himself by providing a suitable specimen of his work, and has been raised to the Degree of Master. To denote this, he now wears his apron as a Master Mason.

He is again blindfolded and a cable tow placed four times about his body, and importantly, divested of metallic substances once again. He undergoes the usual challenges at the door, to emphasize that this Degree is a continuation of the Degrees he has received in Blue Lodge.

The Engraver's Chisel and Mallet

Figure 27 - Engraver's Chisels

This time he is received on the edge of the engraver's chisel, under the pressure of the mallet. He it told that this is to teach him that the moral precepts of the Degree should make a deep and lasting impression upon him. This appears to be another link with the first three Degrees, since instruments are not used to challenge the Candidate in the rest of the Capitular Degrees; also, the gavel (or mallet) is a Working Tool of the Entered Apprentice Degree. It is also uniquely the only time two instruments are used in concert. One should also note that the Engraver's Chisels are a set of chisels with much finer blades than those used for shaping regular stones. These are used for ornamentation and the more subtle work of engraving – in the case of the Keystone the circle and mark of Hiram Abif. The fact that he is now called to a higher and rarer work is reflected in the subtlety of the tools with which he is challenged and presented. This is not the last time he will be challenged, since he will soon move from a position of workman to one of Overseer or Supervisor, where he will be challenged one final time, and this time by an object which is 'neither oblong nor square', so show that he is truly passing to a new level of development.

Later he is explicitly informed that these are also the Working Tools, and that they are used by Master Masons to "cut, carve, mark and indent their work." This is reminiscent of the Entered Apprentice Obligation. The key word is *indent*. Up to now the Masons has been told to create perfect ashlars. Now he is introduced to a more refined tool than the common chisel used for breaking raw stone out of the quarries: he is presented with the engraver's chisel, and implement used to cut *into* the perfect ashlar, in order to place his mark upon it. He is told this to symbolize the refining work of the chisel upon the rough stone, as education refines the mind and ultimately leads him to aspire to the summit of human knowledge.

The description of the mallet is similar to that given for the gavel in the Entered Apprentice Degree, and could suggest it was a carry-over from that Degree.

The Circumambulations

The ceremony continues with the circumambulations. As the Blue Lodge Degree saw the blindfolded Candidate make one, two and three circles about the Altar and past the Senior Officers, so in the Mark Degree he now makes four. His circumambulations are invariably accompanied by pertinent readings from Scripture. Each time he passes the East he halts and gives the due guard and sign of the preceding Degrees; the fourth time he comes to fidelity since he does not yet know the due guard and sign of the fourth (i.e. Mark) Degree.

By proving himself in each of the preceding Degrees he is indicating his mastery over those Degrees, and his worthiness to be received into the next level in the American Degrees.

Figure 28 - The cliff at Joppa or Jaffa

The first scriptural reference comes from Chronicles, and is a description of the transportation of the wood by sea to Joppa. This sets up the pass grip and word.

The next three come from the prophet Ezekiel, Chapter 44, verses 1 – 5. In a way it is an extraordinary passage to use, since Ezekiel prophesied the destruction of the temple, which has not yet been built in the Mark Degree, and how the Prince, High Priest and people must behave to avoid God's wrath. However, the most important part is verse 5, which give rise to the true grip and word of the Degree.

Following the scriptural readings, he is challenged by the Junior and Senior Wardens, as in the preceding Degrees.

The Step and Coming to Order

Again, as in the earlier Degrees, he is now re-conducted to the Senior Warden, and taught how to approach the altar for the fourth time. In doing so he also gives the steps, due guard and signs of the preceding three Degrees. He is brought to the altar and caused to kneel as in the previous Degrees.

This emphasizes the fact that the Mark Degree builds upon the previous Degrees. Indeed, both the Mark and Past Master Degrees take place in a Lodge and are considered part of the telling of the Blue Lodge story. It is not until the Royal Arch Degree that there is a significant movement in both time and circumstance.

The Obligation

The Obligation follows the usual structure. Here much is made of the mark, which is to be expected as a central theme of this Degree. There are three parts to this section. Firstly, he agrees to receive another Brother's mark and grant his request for a loan, or at least to return it with its price, which

Figure 29 - Mason's Mark found in Rosslyn Chapel

is a half shekel of silver. Secondly, he promises not to alter the mark he selects once recorded. Thirdly, he promises he will not lend or sell it, nor pledge it a second time.

This would appear to be a vestige of what might have been a promise made in operative Masonry. It would be important that a Mason didn't cheat by putting someone else's mark on his work. Why would he do this, if his mark ensured his payment? Perhaps it might dissuade him from putting the mark of an enemy upon a poorly executed piece of work in order to get him into trouble? Certainly, one can also see how a Mason fallen upon hard times might be tempted to lend or pledge his mark to another person, since that person could then use it to obtain wages himself, perhaps at a different work site. Finally, one can also see how a Mason might use the mark as a sign of destitution, in order to obtain welfare from fellow Masons.

From a speculative viewpoint, however, the lessons are not to claim work not your own; to extend charity to your Brothers; and to be steadfast in your convictions. As the ritual claims, a Mason's mark was synonymous with his name, so he would no more alter, change, lend or sell his mark than he would his own name.

The penalties may give a Candidate pause for thought. Although a relatively recent development in Freemasonry, the addition of the word 'symbolic' to our Blue Lodge penalties may lead to surprise when the penalties of the American Rite are not 'symbolic' but 'actual.' Of course, they are never carried out, which gives the lie to people who claim the Masons once carried out their penalties. The cutting off of the hand was already enacted in the ritual. However, the cutting off of the ear may refer to an earlier part of ritual now lost over time. The Due Guard, being the cutting off of the ear, may also reference the act of dragging the Candidate by the ear to the Master when he is detected as an imposter, as is practiced in some Lodges.

Another Lesson in Poverty

Almost immediately there is a small play enacted in which there is a knock at the door and an apparently impoverished Brother has his mark presented to the newest member of the Lodge, seeking relief. The Candidate being unable to comply is asked to return the mark with a quarter of a dollar, being the equivalent of a half shekel of silver. Having been divested of metal he cannot comply with this either. At this point all the Brethren offer to help the Candidate fulfill his obligation.

Interestingly, a variation in the oldest ritual in New York, practiced by Ancient Chapter No.1 which was founded some time prior to Webb's codification of the ritual, the Master slips the money into the Candidate's pocket. He is then told to 'seek and ye shall find', a reference to the gospel of Matthew 7:7. He does, and discovers he is not 'entirely destitute' after all.

The similarity of this action with what occurs in the Entered Apprentice Degree, when the Candidate is asked to deposit 'some metallic substance' with the Secretary, is apparent. Indeed, there are many signs which indicate that the Mark Degree developed at least in parallel with the Entered Apprentice Degree, and shared a period of cross-fertilization, resulting in a number of symbols and part of the ritual being common to both. In addition to the request for metallic substance from the Candidate, the reference to "seek and ye shall find" in an early form of the ritual mentioned above is remarkably similar to that section of the Lecture of Reasons in the Entered Apprentice Degree which reminds us that the three distinct knocks given at the door of the Lodge are related to the same passage of scripture. The Due Guard also reminds us of the 'attentive ear' and 'whispering wise counsel into a Brother's ear.'

The Signs, Grips and Words

The first sign is the Grand Hailing Sign or Sign of Distress, and recalls how the Brother was shown to carry and present his work. Being a Sign of Distress, it is not used elsewhere during the ceremony; it is largely added for completeness' sake, since Masons have a far more visible and well-known Sign of Distress given to them in the Third Degree, and no doubt would resort to that one if in trouble. The Principal or 'Heave Over' Sign refers to the rejection of the Keystone, which is made over the left shoulder. The Due Guard and Sign have been explained earlier. These latter three signs need to be known since they are used

Figure 30 - The Harbor at Joppa shows the buildings rising up on what must once have been a steep scarp slope. Joppa - or Jaffa, is immediately South of Tel Aviv in Israel

at the Opening of a Chapter. The pass grip and word derive from the first scriptural reading and the explanation that the wood from the cedars of Lebanon were floated down the coast to Joppa, where the coast was very steep, requiring those on top of the bluff to help the workmen ascend. The harbor is one of the oldest in the world. The password reflects this story, and the grip is what would indeed be used to drag a person upwards. From a symbolic viewpoint, this grip also represents the act of raising a person from one level to a higher one, which is appropriate for a Degree which reminds us that we are advancing further in Masonry.

The real grip and word are taken from Ezekiel, and according to Duncan's Monitor the name is 'Siroc or Mark Well'. The body forms the outline of the letters and the hands now take on a grip which is far less robust than the pass grip. Now, instead of the strong fingers being bound in a grip, the two weakest fingers are locked, perhaps indicating the level of trust between the two Brothers.

Finding the Stone Which Was Lost

At this point in the ceremony three Craftsmen study the plans on the Trestleboard and realize the keystone is missing. It is interesting to note that, while many Mark Lodges use the Overseers for this part of the ritual, this is incorrect: if the Overseers had seen the design they would have immediately recognized both the shape and the mark upon the stone. This review must be performed by three different Brothers, who represent those supervising the work itself; while the Overseers represent an administrative role only.

Figure 31 - Royal Arch Penny

Once the lack of the keystone has been identified, the Senior Warden informs the Right Worshipful Master, who tells the Marshall to 'transmit the mark' to the Senior Warden. The mark he gives him to transmit is one of the coins – the Penny – which will later be given to the Candidates at the end of the ceremony. The Senior Warden uses this to show the assembled Overseers what the stone looks like, and they immediately recognize it as the one they rejected. The fact that the mark needs to be shown to the Senior Warden (Hiram King of Tyre) shows that the only two people who knew what it looked like were King Solomon and Hiram Abif. This may shed more light on the passage from Ezekiel, since it implies that only the King (prince or ruler) was worthy to commune with God an receive the divine plans for His Temple. This idea that the design of the stone was somehow secret or 'hidden' is later reflected in the scriptural verse "to him that overcometh will I give to eat of the hidden manna, and I will give him a white stone, and in the stone a new name written which no man knoweth, saving he that receiveth it." (Revelation Chapter 2, Verse 17).

A search is made and the keystone is found. In some versions the keystone is subtly moved during the preceding part of the ritual, so it is not in the place expected. In other variants it is the Candidate himself who finds it. However, in the Webb version the three Craftsmen locate the stone 'among the rubbish' where it was placed at the start of the ceremony, carry it to the Senior Warden, who compares it to the mark, and has the Overseers carry it up to the Right Worshipful Master. He admonishes the disgraced Overseers with four scriptural readings, each emphasized with blows of the gavel. This is a most powerful moment, and yet it will seem unfair that the Master blames the Overseers who, due to his secrecy, had no idea what the stone would look like.

It is also of note that the scriptural passages refer to the cornerstone, which begins the foundation of a new edifice; while the stone in question is the key stone, which finishes off the building. However, the lessons apply to both, since both are critical to the establishment and endurance of the building. In the Entered Apprentice Degree, the Candidate is told he is a cornerstone and positioned in the Northeast corner of the Lodge. Now he represents the completion of the building, as the symbolic keystone.

It is interesting to note the similarities of this section with the Master Mason Degree. Since we are taught that we are 'living stones', this white stone bearing a person's mark – or name – stands in for that person. As in the Master Mason Degree the stone was thrown into the rubbish, as if dead, by three senior Masons. Its absence was noted and 'strict search' was made for it. On its being found it was carried up to King Solomon who admonished those three who had thrown it over in the first place. Now the worth is recognized, and it will occupy a key position in the Temple.

Figure 32 - Icon of 'The Good Shepherd'

A final point, perhaps, given the Christian roots of many of the Biblical references, is a message of universal hope from the Gospel of Luke 15: 4 – 6. In this the Nazarene talks of the Shepherd who, losing one sheep out of a hundred, nevertheless goes to find it, and when he does he lays it on his shoulders and comes home rejoicing. They say a husbandman can recognize the cry of his animals, even to the individual sheep, goat or cow. Perhaps from this we can draw the hope that, even if we, as a Peculiar Stone, are cast aside and left in the rubbish heap, yet God who knows us and gave us a secret name will come to find us, hear our secret name, and laying us upon his back, return to his kingdom rejoicing that he has found us.

Historical Lecture

The Lecture which follows offers a pause in the action. All are seated and the Master or assigned Brother gives an explanation of the ritual up to this point. He reveals the meaning of the letters on the stone (H∴T∴W∴S∴S∴T∴K∴S). It is noteworthy that these are written in in a circular pattern, between two engraved circles, which once again emphasize the use of the compasses in this second series of Degrees.

Given that this Degree is a combination of two original Degrees, Mark Man which required a Fellowcraft to produce a piece of 'good work, true work, square work', and Mark Master, which required the employment of compasses to produce a keystone, we need to seek what lesson the rejection and rediscovery are trying to teach us.

Figure 33 - Zedekiah's Cave (King Solomon's Quarries)

We must remember that it is not only the Overseers who are ignorant of the function of the keystone. The Candidate is also alleged to have "found it in the quarries and concluding it designed for some portion of the Temple, brought it up." The ritual implies he was working on a regular (i.e. square) piece of work and set that down in order to take this stone instead, since he emphatically tells the Overseers that it is not his own work. The Candidate comes with clean hands.

Why did the Fellowcraft lay down his square stone and pick up a stone which contained elements designed by compasses? We are taught in the Blue Degrees that the compasses represent God (indeed, who can forget the magnificent *Ancient of Days* by William Blake?). While he cannot see the true significance of the keystone, he senses that his development, which up to now has focused on duty, has lacked a *spiritual* element. By gravitating towards a stone which contains arcs and circles, he is reaching out to that spiritual side just as the physical Temple is nearing completion. He is sound in mind and body: now he seeks to work upon his soul. But what of the Overseers? They represent those who mechanically go through the motions, who are accomplished enough in the basic skills but who have not yet grasped the higher purpose of speculative Freemasonry. It also tells us that even the lowly Fellowcraft can rise above his situation and make this journey if he applies himself diligently enough.

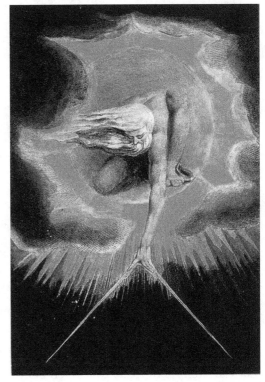

Figure 34 - William Blake: 'Ancient of Days'

At the simplest level, the Degree teaches us that life is fraught with disappointments, and that we must persevere before our initially rejected ideas or actions are finally recognized for what they are, and we finally receive our just reward. But it is man's lot in life to endure hardship, misunderstanding and unjust treatment. In this he reminds us of King David, Solomon's father, who designed the Temple but was forbidden to build it himself. The Address to the Candidate refers to this, and remind him that, even if he is rejected of men and persecuted, he will always find reliable and constant friends among Mark Master Masons, and that his rejected labors will one day be recognized and rewarded.

Figure 35 - As Above So Below

Another theme is that the stone now bears a name or mark. Previously we, as Masons, have labored upon the Spiritual Temple. The Hermetic axiom 'As Above, So Below' has led us to realize that, just as we symbolically build the Temple of stone below, so we are creating that Spiritual Temple not built with hands in heaven; and that our actions on earth will be judged on another plane. We are now sufficiently advanced in our Masonic career to place our name or mark upon our work, so that it will be clearly identified as ours. We now take personal responsibility for our actions.

The lesson on charity is more emphatic in this Degree than in the Entered Apprentice Degree. In that Degree we were asked for some metallic substance to be placed in the annals of the Lodge. However, in this Degree there is a direct and personal application to our charitable nature. This is appropriate at this level, for we are forcibly reminded that we are judged by our actions, and if Charity is the greatest of the theological virtues, the practice of charity will accelerate our success in creating the Spiritual Temple.

In this Degree, much is made of the keystone being the 'stone which was lost but now found', a theme which will be reintroduced in the Royal Arch Degree. Perhaps the most important lesson here is the fact that – especially if we consider the Most Excellent Master Degree as the second part of the Mark Degree – we have the completion of the earthly Temple. Already, while the Temple is nearing completion we see fleeting images of the true purpose of the Masonic cycle: that the Temple must be destroyed and rebuilt within ourselves for us to discover Truth. Hiram is an avatar, and while we watch his death from afar in the Drama of the Master Mason Degree, we dimly perceive that we ourselves must die in order that the germ of Truth within us must grow and blossom. Our contentment with receiving a substitute for Truth in the Master Masons Degree has been gnawing at us, and on finding a stone in the quarry which represents the last step in the earthly Temple and the first step of the spiritual Temple, we run to grasp it, not yet understanding its full meaning, but aware that it is of great importance. We are told that this wisdom is not yet for us, and we return to the quarries to continue work on the earthly Temple. However, our reward later in the Degree is to learn that there is indeed a purely spiritual Temple, and that the stone we found, while being temporarily rejected for the physical Temple, will play a major role in the Temple to come.

Figure 36 - Time braiding the hair of the weeping virgin

Confusion in the Craft

The Lodge is closed in full form, and since work ends at the sixth hour of the sixth day the Senior Warden is again told to pay the Craft their wages. This also becomes an opportunity for the Lodge to distribute Mark Tokens or Pennies, if they employ them. It is a tradition that, once a mark has been selected and registered with the Lodge Secretary in the book of marks, to have that mark engraved in the center of the metal mark. This may be done by an engraver, but since the mark selected should be simple in design and made of straight lines, it is more appropriate if the newly-made Mark Master Mason does it himself. The very act of creating his own Mark Token is a salutary exercise in meditating on the precepts of the Degree.

Figure 37 - Paying the workmen their wages

The Lodge members line up and receive their wages. However, for a second time there is confusion in the Craft (the first was when the keystone was found to be missing). This time the longer-standing members of the Lodge complain that those who have just become Mark Masons are receiving the same pay as them: a penny a day. At this moment, the Right Worshipful Master goes to the altar and reads from the Volume of the Sacred Law. This is a powerful moment, since in the preceding Degrees the Bible has been a powerful, yet static symbol lying upon the altar. Now the Master physically turns the Bible around and reads from Matthew, Chapter 20. The lesson taught is reiterated in the Keystone Lecture.

The story would have been completely familiar to almost all who passed through this Degree a hundred years ago. Sadly, nowadays, this famous parable is rather less known, as is its context. The story itself is about the owner of a vineyard who goes out to find workmen to harvest his grapes. He goes out four times, and at the end of the day pays them all the same wage. Those who labored all day complain that those who only began working in the evening should receive less than them. The owner tells them that he fulfilled his contract with each of them, and that it is his right to do as he will with what is his. And he makes the following point: the last shall be first and the first last.

This passage has vexed commentators for centuries. It is important to read also what comes before, in Matthew Chapter 19. A wealthy young man asks Jesus what more he must do to obtain everlasting life, if he has faithfully obeyed all the Commandments. Jesus replies that he must give away all his wealth. He tells his disciples that a rich man shall not enter the Kingdom of Heaven. At this the disciples ask Jesus who, then, will be saved. He replies that all things are possible through God. Peter then makes an important point. He reminds Jesus that the disciples have indeed given up everything, their wealth, their livelihood and their families to follow him. What then will be their reward? Firstly, Jesus reassures them that their loyalty will be rewarded: "Verily I say unto you, that ye which have followed me in the regeneration, when the Son of Man shall sit in the throne of his glory, ye also shall sit upon twelve thrones, judging the twelve tribes of Israel." Of course, by this Jesus implies that they shall each rule a tribe of Israel (remember Judges were the first rulers of the Children of Israel before they decided they wanted a king to rule over them). But then he adds: "But many that are first, shall be last; and the last shall be first."

Now he tells the parable, which is cautionary, and ends once more with the 'first shall be last' comment. Debates have focused on whether he was referring to the disciples needing to realize that anyone who returns to God before they die shall have an equal inheritance in the Kingdom; or whether he is comforting the disciples by implying that all those Jews who have faithfully followed God through the centuries have no greater claim over the Kingdom than the disciples, who have only followed but a few months. Either way, it is a powerful message, which is reiterated in this section of the ritual.

For us, we perhaps learn that some may have to strive a lifetime to understand the lessons understood by others in only a short time. We do not all develop at the same speed. If we see some younger than ourselves or newer to the Craft grasp points still obscure to us, we must not be tempted to jealousy, or to attack and ridicule those fortunate Masons. We should be content with what we have and strive al the harder to make sense of the symbols and allegories given to us, so that we, too, may understand the divine principles they are intended to portray.

While the attraction of fancy titles and colorful aprons may distract some, the lessons are not in the trappings of Masonry, but in its teachings. True wealth and happiness come from devoting one's time to understanding the meaning behind the rituals, and applying those powerful lessons to our everyday lives. We are also reminded that such inspiration does not come from doing nothing, but through applying ourselves with diligence and a strong sense of duty, building on the strong moral foundation we have hopefully erected during our time in the quarries of the Blue Lodge. This sense of morality provides the foundation upon which the will build our spiritual Temple. *Mens sana in corpore sano.* A healthy mind in a healthy body. Without a strong foundation to withstand the attacks or man and nature, we will labor on our spiritual structure in vain. Now we put our name upon our work, so it will be judged by others, and by the Great Overseer. We have been content with a substitute for the Word, for Truth. Now we will seek the True Word with renewed vigor, for Truth is not a physical, man-made creation, but spiritual, and a divine gift.

Music in the Degree

The Sabbath Ode and the Mark Masters Ode were written by Thomas Smith Webb especially for the Degrees. Webb was an accomplished musician, flute and fife player, singer, composer and conductor. He joined the Boston Philharmonic Society in 1814, becoming its Vice President. He was also a performing member of the Brattle Street Church Choir, and President of the Handel and Haydn Society, conducting a number of concerts for orchestra and voices.

Figure 38 – Sabbath Ode, words by Thomas Smith Webb

Given this interest in music, it is hardly surprising that Webb wrote a number of songs for the Degrees. Recognizing the power of music to add dignity to ritual, while at the same time not wanting to prolong the Degrees, he wrote processional music, to be performed while the Brethren were parading around the Lodge room. Since most Lodges would not have had a musical instrument to hand, and knowing the popularity of singing and music-making at that time, especially within families, his songs, set to well-known tunes, provided an appropriate group activity in the Degrees when no words were being spoken, which punctuated the ritual in appropriate places.

The Sabbath Ode would have provided an opportunity for the Chaplain to show off his solo abilities, while the Mark Masters Ode, sung at the end of the ritual while the Brothers were assembling and processing to collect their wages would have provided a common outlet for the assembled Brethren. The words of both Odes are worth careful reading: they are true poetry.

Biblical References

Of all the Degrees, the Mark Master may contain more biblical quotations than any other – indeed it contains more New Testament quotations than any Degree or Order other than the Templar Orders. This may be partly explained by the fact that we are moving from purely earthly to more spiritual education. Indeed, in his Freemason's Monitor, Webb devotes a significant portion of his comments on the Mark Master Degree to enumerating all the biblical references and reproducing them.

As well as expected quotations from Chronicles (which along with the Book of Kings details the building of King Solomon's Temple), and a couple of quotes from Psalms and Ezekiel, much of the scripture cited is from the New Testament. This may again reflect the probability that the ritual traces its origins in the actual ceremonies used by Operative Masons, which, due to the fact that Christianity was – and is – the established religion of the British Isles, this ensured that any ceremony, in order to meet the approbation of Crown and Church, was liberally sprinkled with passages from the New Testament.

Figure 39 - Thomas Smith Webb Monitor

Be this as it may, the New Testament passages are used sensitively, and only two types of passage are used. Firstly, the parable of the wages paid in the vineyard is used to emphasize a key lesson. Secondly, passages which have sometimes used to draw a parallel between prophetic commentaries in the *Tanakh*, or Jewish Bible, and the Messiah, are here used rather to underscore the passage in the Psalms which talks of the stone the builders rejected becoming the cornerstone. In this context it refers to our own spiritual development as Masons.

The important point is not necessarily which Holy Book is being used, since Freemasonry came into being in a Northern European country where Christianity was the predominant – and official

– religion. The passage extracted are universal in their messages of tolerance, assiduity, self-improvement and charity to others, and are lessons which can be applied by men of all faiths.

And so, the Mark Degree uses symbols, scripture, music, links to prior Degrees, and the usual mixture of drama, lecture and catechism to transmit a powerful message: that in the Capitular Degrees the Brother is going to be transformed from a Master Builder to a Spiritual Builder. In this Degree, he takes the first steps towards the sublime revelations of the Holy Royal Arch Degree.

Figure 40 - Mark Degree Tracing Board (grandchapterofwashington.org)

MMM Quiz #1

1   In what country is the first mention of operative Mark Masons?
(a) England.
(b) Ireland.
(c) Scotland.
(d) North America.

2   How many Officers are there in a Lodge of Mark Master Masons?
(a) 5.
(b) 7.
(c) 8.
(d) 9.

3   Where were the Overseers situated?
(a) In the middle of the room.
(b) South, West and North.
(c) South West and East.
(d) East, North and East.

4   Where did the wood for the Temple come from?
(a) The Quarries of Zaradatha.
(b) The Lebanon.
(c) Joppa.
(d) The Mount of Olives.

5   How did the Craftsmen carry their work?
(a) In their left hand.
(b) Placed upon the palm of the right and left hands.
(c) On their left shoulder.
(d) Between the thumb and fingers of their right hand.

6   What did the Overseers use to test the work?
(a) A Square.
(b) Compasses.
(c) Plumbline.
(d) A Ruler.

7   How did the Overseers dispose of the rejected stone?

(a) Over their left shoulder.

(b) Over their right shoulder.

(c) Over their heads.

(d) Passed from hand to hand.

8   When did the Craftsmen receive their wages?

(a) The sixth hour of the sixth day of the week.

(b) The first hour or the first day of the week.

(c) The third hour of the third day of the week.

(d) The third hour of the sixth day of the week.

9   How did the Senior Warden know the Craftsman seeking wages was not an imposter?

(a) Because he gave the correct pass grip.

(b) Because his hands were dusty and calloused.

(c) Because he gave the correct true grip.

(d) Because he carried a copy of his mark in his hand.

10   How did the Master test the Fellowcraft?

(a) He asked the Master Overseer to obtain the pass.

(b) He asked the Senior Deacon to obtain the pass.

(c) He asked for the pass himself.

(d) He asked for the grip of Fellowcraft.

11   In what manner was the Craftsman found worthy to be taught how to receive his wages?

(a) He could give the pass grip, pass word, true grip and true word of Fellowcraft.

(b) He found the stone which had been thrown over in the rubbish.

(c) He discovered another stone in the quarries.

(d) He presented a piece of his own work which passed the inspection of the Overseers.

12   How was the Candidate received into the Lodge of Mark Master Masons?

(a) While carrying the keystone.

(b) Blindfolded with a cable-tow three times round his body.

(c) By being marked by a chisel.

(d) By giving the pass word at the door.

13   How did the Brethren stand during the Obligation?
        (a) In two parallel lines from the altar to the East.
        (b) They formed a symbolic Temple.
        (c) They stood at their seats at the Sign of Fidelity.
        (d) In a circle about the altar.

14   To whom is a Lodge of Mark Master Masons dedicated?
        (a) God and King Solomon.
        (b) God and Hiram Abif.
        (c) The Grand Geometrician of the Universe.
        (d) The Grand Overseer of the Universe.

15   What does the Candidate promise not to do with the mark which he will hereafter, select once recorded in the Book of Marks?
        (a) Lend or sell it.
        (b) Give it to another Mark Master Mason.
        (c) Pledge it a second time until it has been redeemed form its former pledge.
        (d) Alter or change it.

16   We are told in the ritual that a Brother's work should bear his mark so that it "should be known and distinguished when brought up promiscuously for inspection." What does "promiscuously" mean in this context?
        (a) Carelessly.
        (b) Not in any particular order.
        (c) In a hurry.
        (d) Sexily.

17   What is the origin of the pass grip?
        (a) How the Craftsmen were assisted to climb the sea coast.
        (b) The manner in which the Craftsmen held their axes to fell the trees in the Lebanon.
        (c) A variant of the Master Mason's grip.
        (d) How the Craftsman's hand was grasped at the wicket.

18   How to two Craftsmen form the letters of the true word?
        (a) With their fingers.
        (b) On the five Points of Fellowship.
        (c) At low breath.
        (d) With their arms and legs.

19   Where is the missing keystone?

(a) In the quarries.

(b) In the rubbish.

(c) In Hiram Abif's office.

(d) In King Solomon's apartments.

20   How many letters are upon the keystone?

(a) 6.

(b) 7.

(c) 8.

(d) 9.

21   Why did the Craftsmen cause confusion when they received their wages?

(a) They expected to be paid in shekels.

(b) They expected to be paid more than the new members.

(c) They couldn't find the keystone.

(d) They weren't prepared to abide by the law.

22   What is the stone which was rejected?

(a) The keystone.

(b) The cornerstone.

(c) The perfect ashlar.

(d) None of the above.

23   Who knows the true purpose of the Keystone?

(a) The Overseers.

(b) The Craftsmen with the plans.

(c) King Solomon.

(d) The Candidate.

MMM Discussion Questions

1   Some scholars have put forward the theory that the Mark Man and Mark Master Degrees existed in their own right as an alternative system of Masonic Degrees to the Entered Apprentice and Fellowcraft Degrees (remembering that the Master Mason Degree was a later creation).

       Do you think the Mark Master Mason Degree could serve as a First Degree in Freemasonry if the Entered Apprentice and Fellowcraft Degrees did not exist? What would we gain and what would we lose as lessons?

2   The three Degrees of the Blue Lodge are full of profound teaching, and that no Degree is considered higher than or superior to that of Master Mason. Similarly, the Degrees of the Concordant and Appendant Bodies help to expand upon and explain some of the history and more complex ideas contained in these three Degrees. However, some argue that the Concordant Bodies are unnecessary and a distraction to the teachings of the Blue Lodge Degrees.

       Do you think that your understanding of the Blue Lodge Degrees has been enhanced by going through the Mark Master Degree, or not? Do you think the Appendant Bodies help to expand and explain the messages of the Blue Lodge Degrees?

3   A common concern often expressed in Regular Lodge is that joining the Concordant Bodies takes a Mason away from his Blue Lodge, and makes it more difficult to run the Lodge effectively.

       From your personal experience, have you found that joining Capitular Masonry has made you attend your Blue Lodge less frequently or offered to help less? What about other Masonic friends who are active in Concordant Bodies? Are they more or less active in Blue Lodge since they joined? Either way, why do you think this is?

4   Why did the Craftsman abandon his own work in order to carry someone else's work up to the Overseers? How would you react if you were asked by a friend to do something for him, and then found yourself blamed because it was not the expected action? For example, you might have been asked to check on an elderly relative, who was very unfriendly and unpleasant when you tried to visit with them.

Has this happened to you in real life? How did you feel towards the person who asked you to do them the favor? What was the outcome?

5   The Degree contains many lessons about life and how to life and act. What is the single lesson which was the most important for you? How do you intend to implement that lesson in *your* life?

 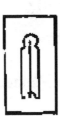 

Virtual Past Master Degree

Background of the Past Master Degree

The origins of the Past Master Degree are lost in history, and it is probably as old as the Entered Apprentice and Fellowcraft Degrees. From what can be gleaned, from the earliest times, when a Master was installed in the Chair to preside over a Lodge, there was a short ceremony, usually performed only in the presence of other Past Masters, in which he possibly took a further Obligation, and was entrusted with a grip and word known only to Past Masters. It is generally believed that this ceremony might have its roots in Operative Lodges, where it would be expected that, given the close attachment to the Church, there would be some kind of ceremony and blessing when a Brother was elected to preside over his Lodge.

Figure 41 - The Earl of Rosslyn

In Scotland, indeed, the Installed Master's Degree was not even introduced until 1870 by the Earl of Rosslyn, from the English Ritual. In a declaration of 1846 it was categorically stated that 'The Grand Lodge further considers every Master Mason qualified to be elected to and fill the chair as R.W. Masons without receiving any additional secrets whatever.'

This sort of Ritual was known by a number of different names, including the Secrets of the Chair, Passing the Chair, Past Master, Passed Master, and Installed Master. The term 'Past Master' is further confused by the fact that a Master-elect could be said to be receiving the Past Master Degree, when the term

Past Master strictly applies to a Master who has served his Lodge for the specified period, and has now vacated the East.

We have learned that the earliest form of the Royal Arch Degree was open only to Past Masters, and it quickly became evident that, given the small number of Past Masters, this important system of teaching Masonic secrets was in imminent danger of becoming extinct. It was among the Antients firstly, that a Degree which conferred the Secrets of the Chair upon worthy and well-qualified Master Masons was worked, which would entitle them to receive the Royal Arch Degree; while the Premier Grand Lodge continued to confer a Past Master Degree upon those elected as Master of their Lodge. Following the Act of Union between the Antients and Moderns in 1813, the United Grand Lodge of England took control and limited the ceremony of Installation to duly elected Masters of Lodges only. From that time the requirement for membership of a Royal Arch Chapter was reduced to being a Master Mason for a determined period of time.

The first documented mention of a Past Master's Degree is found in Anderson's Constitutions of 1723, six years after the founding of the Premier Grand Lodge, but also the time that the first Grand Secretary was appointed, and proper records began to be kept. The first mention of the Past Master Degree in connection with Capitular Masonry was in Bolton, England in 1768, when the minutes mention that nine Brothers received the Royal Arch Degree, despite not having served in the Chair as Master of a Lodge.

Figure 42 - Anderson's Constitutions

In the United Stated, it is believed that the first known mention is the working of the Excellent Degree in St. Andrew's Royal Arch Lodge in 1769, Boston Massachusetts. When St. Andrew's and King Cyrus Chapters met in 1795 to standardize their Chapter Degrees, the records of St. Andrew's Chapter reported the working of the Past Master and Most Excellent Master Degrees in place of their Excellent and Super Excellent Degrees. Many scholars are certain this simply reflects a name change, and that this indicates the Excellent Degree practiced by them was in fact a Past Master Degree.

Naturally, given that the Past Master Degree was adopted as part of the series of Capitular Degrees by General Grand Chapter, there was occasional tension with those Grand Lodges who practiced a Past Master Degree as part of its Lodge Installation ceremonies. In 1853, the Triennial Session of General Grand Chapter resolved: "This body does not claim jurisdiction over the degree of Past Master, when about to be conferred on a Master-elect of a subordinate Lodge.

Figure 43 - Early engraving of a ribald event

Nature – and the inventive Mason – abhors a vacuum, and during the 1800s it appears the Degree of Past Master become increasingly elaborate and ribald, finally leading the General Grand Chapter under its General Grand High Priest, Charles Gilman of Maryland, to revise the Ritual in 1856. Albert Gallatin Mackey, his successor, commented in his Book of the Chapter (pub. 1858): "One of the evils resulting from the disseverance of the Past Master's degree from its legitimate position as a part of the installation service in a symbolic lodge, was the introduction of a number of ceremonies into the Chapter degree... At length a powerful effort was made to divest the degree of those offensive ornaments which had been gradually fastened upon it, and to restore it, as nearly as possible, to its original simplicity."

That the Degree had become 'offensive' was reflected by Edmund Ronayne, writing in his 1879 exposé of Freemasonry: "Notwithstanding this recommendation, the subordinate Chapters throughout the country continued to indulge in almost unlimited buffoonery in conferring this degree... I received this degree of Past Master twice, first in the Chapter on which occasion all kinds of stupid horse-play were indulged in at my expense..."

The revised Ritual intended "to abridge the ceremonies now conferred in the Past Master's degree within the narrowest constitutional limits, only retaining the inducting of the candidate into the Oriental Chair, and communicating the means of recognition."

The current ritual reflects this minimalism, and the Degree is comparatively short, certainly in comparison with the now elaborate ritual conducted by a Board of Past Masters in the English Emulation Ritual. While some States no longer confer any kind of Past Master Degree, New York still holds a Board of Installed Masters in a side room prior to installing the Master-elect of a Symbolic Lodge, at which he takes his Obligation and is entrusted with the Grip and Word of Past Master.

Unusually, the Past Master Degree performed by Ancient Chapter No. 1 in New York may still contain some of the elements referred to by Mackey, since the Ritual includes a short scene which most certainly places the Candidate seated in the Oriental Chair in an embarrassing situation. Of course, what may have been considered ribald at the time is now seen as a quaint preservation of historical ritual!

In 1942, an additional part to the Degree, called The Allegory, composed by E∴ Howard, L. M. Jones, Past High Priest of Unity Chapter No. 16 located in Dayton, Ohio was approved for optional adoption in the Virtual Past Master Degree by General Grand Chapter; and it is included in the Appendix to this Course.

Differences between an Actual and Virtual Past Master

Given that a Past Master Degree is practiced within a Chapter, however similar it may be in form to that practiced within the Blue Lodge system, in 1853, it was categorically declared to be unconnected with the latter Degree, as it was necessary to distinguish between the two forms of Past Master Degree practiced in Capitular and Symbolic Masonry.

Some research has suggested that there may at one time have been differences in the secrets conferred, either a slight variation in grip or password, to ensure that nobody receiving the Past Master Degree as a prelude to receiving the Royal Arch Degree could gain entrance to a Lodge of Past Masters about to confer their version upon a Master-elect. In the United States, at least, this possible difference, if it ever existed, has disappeared over time, and there is now no substantial difference between the two Rituals, other than the fact that, in the Blue Lodge setting, obedience to the Grand Lodge, its Constitutions, Laws and Edicts is sworn; and the ancient penalties are omitted. Also, only the grip and word are given. In Blue Lodge, the Charge, and the presentations of gavel, Constitutions, Charter and gavel are done in presence of the whole Lodge at the Installation Ceremony (and sometimes non-Masonic visitors if an open Installation is conducted).

Another difference is in the name. While the ceremony within a Lodge created a Past Master (sometimes referred to as an Actual Past Master), the ceremony within Capitular Masonry creates a Virtual Past Master. This is to indicate that he has not been elected by a Lodge to serve over them, nor has he been required to meet the other prerequisites such as having served as a Warden. Because of this he cannot serve as a Master in a Blue Lodge, nor expect to receive any of the rights and privileges associated with that honor. These include conferring the Entered Apprentice, Fellowcraft or Master Mason Degrees, being invited to a seat in the East, or being received in a Blue Lodge as a Past Master. Similarly, many of the duties of a Past Master recited in the Chapter are not in fact relevant to a Virtual Past Master (such presiding at dedications, consecrations, the laying of cornerstone, and presiding at funeral services).

Variations Can Lead to Embarrassing Situations!

Figure 44 - The Three Principals

Unfortunately, the variations in requirements to receive – and to observe – the Royal Arch Degree can lead to embarrassment when visiting other countries. For example, while any American Master Mason can, by virtue of receiving the Virtual Past Master Degree, receive the Royal Arch Degree, and thereby rise through the offices to become High Priest of his Chapter, in England and Ireland, while any Master Masons may become a Royal Arch Mason, only those who have sat as Master of a Lodge may be elected to the three principle positions of the Council – Scribe, King or High Priest. An English Mason would find it most confusing that an American Mason could be a Past High Priest yet not Past Master of a Lodge. Another source of much confusion is that, in the Domatic Ritual (practiced in England and her Commonwealth, including Canada), the Grand

Council are called the Three Principal Officers – and the most senior one is 'Z', or Zerubbabel the King. 'J' or Jeshua the High Priest is the second in line. And the sign given on entering and retiring is uniquely given with the *left*, and not the right hand in the English Royal Arch!

Figure 45 - A Threefold Cord

This can lead to problems when an English Royal Arch Mason wishes to visit an American Chapter. In theory, there are a few areas of concern. Firstly, if he is not a Past Master, he will not have received the Past Master Degree – and indeed in most jurisdictions receiving the Past Master Degree in a Blue Lodge is for some reason not considered a substitute for receiving the 'expedient' version in the Capitular Degrees! Secondly, since it is an entirely separate Body, he may not be a Mark Master Mason. Finally, since the Most Excellent Master Degree forms part of what we call the Cryptic Council, he probably won't have received that either.

A key issue is the fact that only Past Masters can invoke the Great and Sacred Name under a Living Arch and over a Triangle. In English Chapters, the three Principal Officers raise the Arch, give the words and lower the Arch while the rest of the Companions watch. An English Royal Arch Mason is therefore not equipped to participate in our Openings and Closings.

The situation is similarly confusing for the English visiting a Scottish Chapter. Not only are the Mark and Excellent Master Degrees prerequisites, the English Royal Arch Mason will not be permitted into the Chapter until he was 'taken the Veils', since the Ceremony of the Veils only exists in a 'time immemorial' ritual confined to a few Lodges in Bristol, and the Domatic Ritual practiced elsewhere does not use veils. On the other hand, the fact that the Scottish Constitution does not require one to be a Past Master in order to receive – or confer – the Royal Arch Degree, has also led to some difficult situations in the past, since this creates a situation in which a High Priest who has neither sat as Master of a Lodge nor received the Virtual Past Master Degree can confer the Royal Arch Degree, whose validity would be questioned both under the English and General Grand Chapter Constitutions!

There are just a few examples of the many differences which can lead to embarrassment, or possibly worse, a violation of our own Obligations if we allow those who have not yet taken certain Obligations to see the working and receive the signs and words. In all cases it is best to contact the Grand Secretary's Office to double check the situation regarding a visitor, if any notice of an impending visit has been given. In the New York Jurisdiction, a recent change was made to the Constitution to ensure the Mark, Past Master, Most Excellent Master and Royal Arch Degrees are given in that order: yes, it was discovered that a Chapter had conferred the Degrees in a random order!

The General Grand Chapter has a provision in its Constitution that if a person presents himself from another jurisdiction as a Royal Arch Mason, he may receive the preceding three Degrees in order to heal him and allow him to attend a meeting of Chapter without charge or capitation fee. However, this is impractical in most instances, since the visitor probably would not be around for the length of time required to put on the Mark, Past Master and Most Excellent Master Degrees.

When investigating a prospective visitor to a Chapter, if they hail from a jurisdiction other than one under the auspices of General Grand Chapter, you now understand that there are a number of precautions which must be taken, all the while ensuring that you in no manner offend the prospective visitor. If, for example, the visitor is a Principle or Past Principal, he may be invited to attend the conferral of the Royal Arch Degree. It is up to the High Priest whether a visitor who is not a Past Master should be allowed to attend a Royal Arch Degree, and in any event, he may only observe, and not participate in the ceremony. Nobody outside the jurisdiction of the General Grand Chapter should attend the Opening and Closing of a Royal Arch Lodge, since they will not be in possession of the intervening signs and due guards of the 4th to 7th Degrees.

If a person has moved to the United States and intends to affiliate with a Chapter, it is best if they simply go through the Degrees here, so that they might be best prepared to both learn all the Signs and Due Guards, and so that the Certificate they receive will allow them free entry into any Chapter under the purview of the General Grand Chapter.

Lessons of the Past Master Degree

The Address to the Candidate expressly states that: "The Past Master's Degree, unlike all the other Degrees in Freemasonry, sheds no light upon itself." It later states: "Our candidates are made to pass the Chair simply as a preparation and qualification towards being invested with the solemn instructions of the Royal Arch."

However, it would not be strictly accurate to say that undergoing a ceremony which, symbolically at least, prepares you to preside over a Lodge is without teaching. Whether or not the Candidate actually has to go through the work of planning and running an efficient Lodge, the very act of taking an Obligation, and focusing on the accoutrements with which he is furnished provide a number of points for meditation.

Indeed, it is to be hoped that there is something to be learned in this Degree. The Address tells us that "it was doubtful to many if it (the Past Master Degree) could legally be abolished, and, the law still requires that the August degree of Royal Arch shall be restricted to Part Masters." However, this statement is not strictly true, since a number of jurisdictions have removed the Degree yet their members are still recognized by jurisdictions which have not. It would also seem tragic if what was considered a meaningless ceremony was blindly followed from century to century which had no discernible use at all, simply because of blind tradition.

One author has described the lesson inculcated in this Degree as "responsible leadership." It teaches that moderation, decorum and justice are essential for the fair exercise of Masonic leadership, and since the Capitular Degrees are intended to make the Brothers ever more tied to the beloved Craft and teaches them to lead their younger and less enlightened Brethren through leadership, example and education, this Degree would seem to be a moment of stillness for the Candidate to reflect upon those important attributes.

The emblem of the square is worn about the neck, rather than being presented to him as a Working Tool or indicated upon the Holy Bible. It is to remind the Master forcibly that it is upon himself he must work to create the spiritual temple. He must take up the work and assume it himself in order to lead by example.

The threefold cord is likewise a reminder that, while the follower offers of himself, he must offer twice as much to help the newly-made Masons to achieve his goals. In some interpretations, it manifests a lesson indicated earlier – the Capitular Degrees emphasize a

Figure 46 - An English Past Master's Jewel, including the 47th Proposition of Euclid

transition from the physical basis of the Symbolic Degrees to a Spiritual nature. Thus the Master offers an addition, spiritual level to the grip to raise the Candidate up to a higher plane.

In particular, it reminds us that we are bound by three kinds of law: the Law of Self, the Law of Man, and the Law of God.

The Law of Self is that circumscribing of passions we learned in the First Degree, the need to control ourselves in order to make us fit citizens of society and a help to our fellow man.

The Law of Man is represented by the presentation of the Constitutions and Bylaws, which teach us that, as members of society, we should both abide by and as Master enforce those rules which mankind has commonly agreed to follow.

Finally, by pointing once more to the Volume of the Sacred Law and invited to study and follow its precepts, we are reminded that the most sublime Law is God's, and if all our actions are calculated to do His will, we will never falter.

Figure 47 - The Past Master

VPM Quiz #2

1   Where did the Past Master Degree originate?
(a) With the Moderns.
(b) With the Antients.
(c) With the Irish.
(d) We don't really know.

2   What was believed to be the original purpose of the Past Master Degree?
(a) A means to obtain the Royal Arch Degree.
(b) A way of honoring and distinguishing a Master of a Lodge.
(c) A ritual descended from the Knights Templar in Scotland.
(d) A ritual recognizing the service of a retiring Stonemason.

3   Who were the Giblim?
(a) Overseers.
(b) Stonesquarers.
(c) Woodcarvers.
(d) Metalworkers.

4   The Degree of Past Master has been…
(a) A ceremony to install the Master-elect of a Lodge.
(b) A ceremony to permit a Master Mason to receive the Royal Arch Degree.
(c) A ceremony designed to haze and embarrass a fellow Mason.
(d) All of the above.

5   The first working of the Past Master Degree was…
(a) At St. Andrew's Royal Arch Lodge in Boston.
(b) At Kilwinning Lodge in Scotland.
(c) At a Bolton Lodge in England.
(d) Unknown.

6   What three laws have some researchers suggested the Degree promotes?
(a) Self, Man and God.
(b) Lodge, Chapter and God.
(c) Earthly, Spiritual and Heavenly.
(d) Torah, New Testament and Koran.

7 Who is covered in a Past Master's Lodge?
(a) The Right Worshipful Master.
(b) Everyone present.
(c) The Candidate.
(d) The Right Worshipful Master *or* the Candidate.

8 Which jurisdictions listed below currently require a Candidate for the Royal Arch to have received the Virtual Past Master Degree?
(a) England.
(b) Ireland.
(c) United States.
(d) All the above.

VPM Discussion Questions

1   What do you think about the Virtual Past Master Degree? Should there be a Degree which gives away the Secrets of the Chair to a person who hasn't served as Worshipful Master? Should we have the Degree at all – couldn't the United States simply follow other countries and allow anyone who is a Master Mason to become a Royal Arch Mason without going through the Past Master Ceremony?

2   We now have a Past Master Degree which, according to the revision in 1856, limits the action to installing the Candidate and giving him the grip and word. Indeed the ritual tells us that this Degree "sheds no light upon itself." Do you think this is a wasted opportunity? If you were allowed to rewrite the Ritual in order to inculcate further Masonic light or instill a moral lesson, what would it be? What would you add to the Ritual?

3   The (New York) Constitution currently states in Article V, Section 505.3: "One who has not received the degree of Past Master under the auspices of a Chapter cannot be permitted to be present in a Past Master's Lodge opened under a Royal Arch Warrant." Given the origin of the Virtual Past Master Degree, do you think we should recognize an Actual Past Master going through the Capitular Degrees as such, or does it make sense to have him go through the Virtual Past Master Degree?

Most Excellent Master Degree

Brief History

The Symbolic Degrees are set in the nearly competed Temple of King Solomon, as is the Mark Degree. The more elaborate Actual Past Master's Degree, as practiced in England at least from the mid-1800s, and in the longer explanation in the Ritual practiced in some States, is set in the Temple at a time following its completion and dedication, and describes the visit of the Queen of Sheba to see the Temple with her own eyes. In the Royal Arch Degree we will move forward several hundred years in history to a time when Solomon's Temple lies in ruins. Masonry abhors a vacuum, and it was perhaps inevitable that at some point a ritual would be written which covered perhaps the most important moment in the story of King Solomon's Temple: its completion and dedication.

Figure 48 - 'Solomon and the Queen of Sheba' by Giovanni Demin

There is a symbolic and esoteric reason why this story needed to be told, too. How are we to move from the story of an incomplete Temple which is meant to represent that Temple we are building within ourselves, to the rebuilding of the Second Temple and discovery of Truth, if we never completed the first task?

Given these facts it would be quite easy to believe in the long-told story that it was Thomas Smith Webb who penned the Ritual for Most Excellent Master, in order to create the perfect conclusion to the Blue Lodge system and the transition into the Red Degree of Holy Royal Arch. Indeed, that is what many researchers both assumed and wrote in their books. However, the story is far more complicated than that.

In the previous session we learned that St. Andrew's Royal Arch Lodge conferred the Excellent Master Degree, which is believed to be an early form of the Past Master Degree. However, they also conferred a Degree called the Super Excellent Master (not to be confused with the Degree of the same name conferred in a Cryptic Council). The name 'Excellent' was already used in several Degrees in existence in the mid-1700s. While a number of members had connections with Irish Masonry, which included Degrees with names such as 'Excellent' and 'Super Excellent', there is a likely candidate in the 19th Degree of the Scottish Early Grand Rite, called 'Most Excellent Master', which closely resembles our present Degree. The Candidate is admitted on the Keystone, and the Most Excellent Master who presides tells the Candidate: "This degree was founded to commemorate the finishing of the first Temple…" It is the conclusion of the authors of the official history of the Royal Arch

Figure 49 - Frontispiece of the Geneva Bible of 1560

Degrees, commissioned by the General Grand Chapter, that this is the most probable source of the Most Excellent Master Degree, despite the fact that there is no clear trail showing how the Degree traveled from Scotland to America. They add the interesting comment that the name 'Excellent' almost certainly came from the Geneva Bible (which was commonly in use in the colonies at the time, alongside the King James Bible, from a footnote to I Kings, 5:18 which said: "The Ebrew worde is Giblim which some say, were excellent masons" (*sic*).

Also of note, while the Degree might have come from Scotland, the Degree called 'Excellent' in their system nowadays is a required precursor to receiving the Royal Arch Degree, but its Ritual now encompasses the Passing of the Veils. It was also noted above that some researchers believe the Most Excellent Master Degree may originally have been a part of an extended version of the Mark Degree, in which the Keystone, having been lost and found, was then used to complete the Temple.

Whatever its origin, it was not the original work of Thomas Smith Webb. Records show that, in 1783, St. John's Lodge No. 2 in Middletown, Connecticut formed a Chapter, at which several members were introduced into the "sublime degree of most excellent Masons." However, the records show the ceremony took no longer than 30 minutes, which would scarcely have allowed time to place the Keystone, and certainly not enough time to perform the Dedication Ceremony.

In 1797 Temple Chapter, a Royal Arch Chapter, was founded in Albany by Webb and others, with Webb being installed as High Priest. At the following meeting, in mid-February, five Candidate (Ezra Ames among them) had the Degree of Most Excellent Master conferred upon them. However, Webb and his colleague, John Hanmer had already learned of this Degree in 1796, when they visited Cyrus and St. Andrew's Chapters. The version they observed and recorded was the shorter one which only included the placing of the Keystone. While not the author of the Most Excellent Master Degree, most researchers are confident that he was the ritualist who expanded the Degree into its present form, including the important processions and the Dedication of the Temple.

Figure 50 - Interior of Old Convention Hall, Kansas City

While this Degree can be performed with dignity by a relatively small cast, it has always been the one which has attracted the most opulent performances. Of course, modern laws forbid the burning of incense or the lighting of banks of candles in many locations, and in particular the extravagant pyrotechnics which were the culmination of this Degree, when the Shekinah descended from heaven to light the pot of incense. In 1922 in the old Convention Hall in Kansas City, Missouri, in the presence of the General Grand High Priest, Dr. William Frederick Kuhn, over *one thousand* Candidates received the Degree before an audience of over *eight thousand* Companions. A seventy-five piece orchestra and one hundred fifty-strong choir provided the music; and the processions contained between two to three hundred participants! However, the opulence of the Ritual should not take away from the important message: that one cycle has ended and a new cycle – a more spiritual one – is about to begin.

Purpose of the Degree

The Degree is what is sometimes called a 'pivot Degree', in that it completes one story cycle and prepares for the next cycle. Indeed, in mainland Europe the Royal Arch has played such a role in the past: in both the Rite of Strict Observance of Baron von Hund and the Scottish Rectified Rite of Jean-Baptiste Willermoz in the late 1700s, both being Christian Orders, the Royal Arch story was used to lead the candidates from the Old Testament stories to the New Testament. Hiram was depicted as having risen from the dead, as an Exemplar for all Masons who, having completed the physical Temple, now needed to see it torn down – symbolized by Hiram's death – in order to rise again from the ruins and discover Truth, which was symbolized by Hiram's resurrection.

In this sense, the preceding Degrees are now crowned by this final scene. As participants in the building of the Temple, the Craftsmen who discovered the assassins, who marked their work and received wages, and who were installed as Masters, as the Overseers of other more junior Workmen, and who thereby proved their proficiency in all the preceding Degrees, are finally recognized as Most Excellent Masters. We have completed our labors upon the physical Temple in the physical Sphere, and are now going to Graduate, in a sense, before taking up more spiritual labors. In this Degree we physically enact a great spiritual Truth: the

Figure 51 - Hiram rising from his tomb (from the Degree of Scottish Master of St. Andrew)

completed Temple is now fit to house the Ark of the Covenant, just as our Great Work upon ourselves – that work of spiritual alchemy – has transformed ourselves from rough, crude stones into a Temple of holiness and morality fit to house the Divine Spark of Truth.

Since then the one major change made to the Ritual in many States has been the elimination of the Most Excellent Masters Song, penned by Webb himself. We are fortunate in New York that the song is still included in our Ritual. Every attempt should be made to sing it: the best tune to use is O Come All Ye Faithful (*Adeste Fideles*), since many people know the tune. The penultimate line needs to be repeated three times. If that is not possible, if there is a soloist of any worth in the Chapter, they may sing it as a solo. The atmosphere then becomes more powerful for the focus it brings to the ceremony.

The Six Circumambulations

Following the admission, there is a challenge, in which he candidate is tested with the Keystone. Having carried it as someone else's work in the Mark Degree, now he is finally identified with it himself. This symbolizes the fact that he is now passing to a higher level, and as this Most Excellent Master Degree represents, in a way the second turn of the cycle of development, so in this Degree, which follows the usual form of all the preceding Degrees (with the exception of the Past Master

Degree, which requires no challenge at the door of the Lodge), we can see the progression of tools and objects with which the candidate is challenged tells its own story.

The Profane entering the Lodge is challenged with no particular instrument, other than being told that it is sharp. In England, it is a dagger or poignard; but the important thing is that it is sharp and he feels it. There are many meanings to this symbol, from the prick of conscience to the simpler barring entrance.

However, once he becomes a Mason, he is challenged with a progression of implements, from the Square, then the Compasses, then the Engravers Chisel, and finally here the Keystone. This is no random progression. His first challenge is with the symbol of the Terrestrial World – the Square. Then he is challenged by the symbol of the Grand Architect and the Celestial World – the Compasses, as he completes his journey through the Blue Lodge Degrees. Next he is challenged by the Chisel which, as we have seen, begins to hint at the internal world and the beautification of the work. He is now in symbolic possession of all the implements required to cut and prove the Keystone, for which his labors on the perfect ashlar are shown to be but a preparation. By mastering both himself and the lessons of the previous Degrees he is finally allowed to be touched by – or represent – the Keystone, that Peculiar Stone which completes the Temple, whose base is firmly seated on a terrestrial foundation, and whose cap or 'cape' extends upwards like a rainbow, striving towards the heavens. And upon this Peculiar Stone is written a Name…

Figure 52 - Moslems circumambulating around the Ka'aba

This time he circumambulates, or circles six times clockwise about the Altar, pausing before the Right Worshipful Master each time to salute with the sign and due guard of each ascending Degree. At each circumambulation, the Chaplains recites verses from Psalm 24, which tradition says: "accompanied a ceremony of the entry of God (invisibly enthroned upon the Ark) into the Temple." (United States Conference of Catholic Bishops).

Now the number six – and the number seven – have great symbolic significance in the Bible. God created the heaven and the earth in six days, and on the seventh He rested. In our Ritual we perform six circumambulations, and the ceremony of completion ends with the placing of the Keystone signifying the work is done. We are told to remove our aprons. In other words, we rest. We have built our Temple in six days, and now man has been perfected, there is rest.

The theme can also be seen in the Book of Joshua, when the Israelites circumambulate the city of Jericho in silence for six days, and on the seventh circumambulate seven times with shouting and noise. We can also see the movement in the Hajj, when Moslems circumambulate the Ka'aba – this time anticlockwise – seven times. In each Degree the Candidate has circumambulated, or walked in a circle, one extra time for each higher Degree. It should be recognized that in most religions and magical practices the act of circumambulating is symbolic of raising energy or rising to a higher plane. This is the principle, for example, behind walking labyrinths, which we can see in many cathedrals, as well as outdoor groves.

Figure 53 - Joshua and the Walls of Jericho

Once accomplished, the Candidate approaches the Altar to take the Obligation.

The Obligation, Penalty, Grip and Word

Once the Candidate is in due form, the Companions gather in a circle about him, emphasizing that peculiar symbol of the point with a circle – now physically represented by the Altar and Candidate within the Fraternal Circle of his Brethren, just as the Brethren formed the Symbolic Temple in the Blue Lodge at the time of taking the Obligation. The Square has become a circle; and the Brethren now symbolize that circle first seen in the Mark Master Degree upon the Keystone.

The most important part of the Obligation, which otherwise follows the usual formula, is that of promising "to dispense true Masonic light and knowledge to my less informed Brethren to be best of my ability." Having become proficient in the knowledge of all the preceding Degrees, the Brother promises to become a beacon, or a mirror, to reflect that Light and Knowledge upon other worthy Masons.

It is interesting that the penalty this time emphasizes the removal of the organs of physical life and their being thrown back onto the earth to rot (the term 'dunghill' is poetically used). In other Degrees an offending part of the anatomy was usually removed – for example, the right hand in the Mark Degree for improperly seeking wages not one's due – but here the element is that of Earth. We will return to this later.

The Grip is called the 'Cover Grip' since it covers, or includes, all the preceding grips (really it only covers the Entered Apprentice, Fellowcraft and Master Mason grips – but we shall see why in the section below called 'Esoteric Implications').

The Word, 'Giblim', means 'Most Excellent Master' according to the Geneva Bible, as we have read. As such the title means little in itself in the English language, since it is but an honorific, and is used in the preceding Degree. However, the Hebrew word 'Rabboni' makes a powerful statement. It is only used once in a footnote in the Old Testament, and but twice in the New Testament. It can also mean 'My Great Master', and is the term uttered by Mary Magdalene upon seeing the resuscitated Jesus. It was also used by the blind man in Mark 10:51 when he asks Jesus to restore his sight. We must remember that both Operative and Speculative Masonry developed in countries where Christianity was the predominant – if not sole – religion. It is hardly surprising, therefore to find this word taking on a much stronger meaning. So in the Bible the word is never actually used to indicate a good craftsman: it *is* used to indicate a man considered to be without sin; in this context the word becomes a very powerful statement indeed. Again, in many continental rituals of a Christian nature, Hiram becomes Christ, and of course one famous name for Christ is – the *Word*.

The Completion of the Temple

Figure 54 - The Keystone set in place

This theme has been comprehensively covered already. The only point to be made here is that the anthem tells us "to bring forth the cape-stone". Now, the copestone, or capstone is the final stone which tops off a building. It is **not** the Keystone, for that *keys* an arch together. In most States, the word has been modified to say 'Keystone'. Albert Mackey, former General Grand High Priest, makes much of this point in his Monitor. Perhaps the confusion is deliberate: the Keystone has an important significance due to its shape, and its central position in the Arch, which has often been portrayed as holding up the canopy of heaven like the arch of Noah's rainbow, perhaps therefore harking back to the Mark Mariner Degree, the stones forming the zodiacal signs between the Solstices which at one time marked the six monthly term of the Lodge Master in a number of traditions. On the other hand, the Capstone marks the true completion of a building, yet its shape is of little interest, since it could be just another rectangular ashlar.

Removal of Aprons

The removal of Aprons is a powerful symbol that we have come to the end of the Symbolic Degree cycle. It also represents that seventh day of rest, referred to above. Everything in this Degree emphasizes and stresses completion, and end of a cycle and the beginning of a new one. But to proceed from one cycle to the next it is important that one has learned the lessons of the previous one.

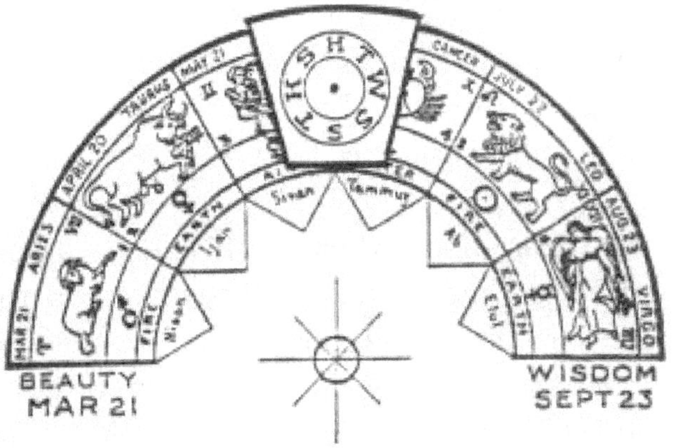

Figure 55 - Arch and Keystone related to the Zodiacal Signs

In the circumambulations of this Degree we were reminded of Creation. Indeed, many papers have been written linking the building of the Temple with the story of Creation. Consider again the number 'seven'. The Temple was 'seven years and upwards' in its construction (in Leviticus 25:4 the seventh year is called a Sabbath, which was the day God rested). It was dedicated during the Feast of Tabernacles, a seven-day festival held in the seventh month.

In the context of Creation, what could removing one's apron symbolize? Genesis 3:7 says: "And the eyes of them both were opened, and they knew that they were naked; and they sewed fig leaves together, and made themselves aprons." Note that in this case the Geneva Bible is most definitely *not* referenced: it is also known as the 'Breeches Bible' since it says they made themselves breeches! So a key external symbol of man's fall and imperfection is the wearing of the apron. Yet once the work upon ourselves is completed we remove the apron. We have in a way atoned – we have returned to our original, or primitive, state. We have created a Temple fit for the Lord to dwell in.

Figure 56 - Adam and Eve chased from Eden

Once more we see a reference to the fact that we have completed the external work, and are now ready for the internal work which will be our task in the next level, plane, or phase of our development.

Interestingly, there are a few States where the aprons are not removed, for example Maine and Minnesota. However, the removal is Standard Work in New York.

The Reception

In this Degree, there is no conferral of special secrets, nor any teachings to be imparted. It is assumed the Most Excellent Master already knows all he needs to, and this is more of a 'Graduation Ceremony'. Therefore, King Solomon and Hiram, King of Tyre do not confer a Degree, but rather greet the newly-Obligated Brethren, receiving and acknowledging them Most Excellent Masters.

But this is once more accomplished through touch. In every Degree, more or less subtle depending upon the source of the Ritual, there is a transmission, accomplished through a meeting of bodies, a handshake. Think how all rituals of transmission, adulthood, religious passage are always accompanied by the passing of a 'certain something' from the person who has it to the person who does not, by means of touch. We offer our hand "in token of

Figure 57 - The acknowledgement of equality

friendship and Brotherly love". We shake hands, we embrace, we kiss, we impose hands upon the head, and we anoint: all involve touching. This time the handshake is given and received as equals, not with one person kneeling. The acknowledgement is therefore of a peer.

The Dedication of the Temple

Figure 58 - Dedication of the Temple

The Dedication is almost completely made up of readings from II Chronicles Chapters 5 and 6. Those parts narrating history are usually given to the Chaplain, but the portentous prayer of King Solomon at the Dedication is put in his mouth and is followed by what used to be one of the most dramatic moments of all Freemasonry (prior to fire hazard laws, that is!).

Following the deposit of the Ark of the Covenant in its proper place, and the invocation by King Solomon, the sign of divine approbation – possibly even a sign of the Lord coming down to occupy the Mercy Seat – used to be a most dramatic pyrotechnic display to visibly indicate the Shekinah coming down from heaven and igniting the incense. II Chronicles is a little more prosaic, telling us that "the house was filled with a cloud."

This 'fire from heaven' is a common manifestation of communication between God and man. To give some example,

Figure 59 - Elijah and the priests of Ba'al

think of the fire which lit the altar built by Abraham on which to sacrifice his son; the destruction of Sodom and Gomorrah, the pillar of fire of the Exodus; the burning bush. Following this manifestation, we have the fire Elijah summoned down on the guard and his fifty men, and of course the fire which descended to light the bituminous substance drawn up by the priests and laid upon the altar at the time of the Rededication of the Second Temple of Zerubbabel. Further, we have the tongues of fire which settled upon the Disciples. Each of these indicate a moment of communication between God and His creation. It also suggests that the Ark of the Covenant was someone inactive until that moment, in that the true sign of occupancy or divine approbation did not take place until the divine fire descended, and only then was the Holy of Holies truly filled with the glory of God. If the analogy between Man and the Temple as a type of Man is to be maintained, then it is not until the divine breath or Word enters the body that it is vivified with the spirit.

Psalm 122 is then spoken antiphonally (i.e. alternating verses) between King Solomon and Hiram King of Tyre. This unusual treatment of the Psalm is more at home in religious services, where choirs often sing antiphonally (the two choirs being called *Cantoris*, or the side where the Cantor is seated, usually in the North, and *Decani*); or the congregation reads verses antiphonally with the priest. This could reflect the idea of speaking in tongues. When God communicated with Moses out of the burning bush, Moses complained he did not have the gift of rhetoric, and God appointed Aaron, his Brother, to speak for him. Similarly, in the New Testament, when the fire descended the Disciples began to speak in tongues. Here, the words of peace are alternated between two Kings who, for one short moment, become one.

The Address

The Address to the Candidate is most comprehensive and gives a detailed account of the ritual which preceded it. Perhaps the most interesting part is the last sentence, which is truly a harbinger of what will follow: "…that when we leave this, for that far distant country from whence we shall never return, we may there receive the wages of faithful craftsmen."

We will not seek material wages in that distant land; for surely the only 'wage' we seek is the True Word? And yet we have to leave this land for that in order to receive it. At the Opening of Lodge, the Senior Warden says he became a Master Mason "to obtain the Maser's Word, travel in foreign lands, work and receive a Master's wages?" But does he mean the *True* Word of Master Masons, and not the Substitute Word? Could this mean he has to travel to a far distant country in order to obtain that Word? And we know that far distant country from whence we shall never return is across the veil of death. Must we die, then, before we can learn the Truth?

The Temple as Creation / The Temple as Man

The building of the Temple holds much deeper symbolism than providing useful tools for us to consider when trying to improve ourselves.

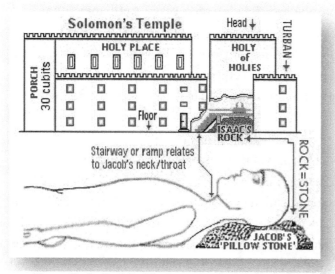

Figure 60 - by Tony Badillo (see www.templesecrets.info)

Many religious commentators, both Jewish and Christian, have been struck by the parallel between the story of Creation in Genesis and the building of the Temple in 2 Chronicles. Once more the number '7' is highlighted. In his paper *Creation as Temple-Building and Work as Liturgy in Genesis 1-3* by Jeff Morrow of Seton Hall University, he notes that Genesis 1:1 contains '7' words in Hebrew. Genesis 1:2 has fourteen – '7 x 2'. Other important words in the text may be counted in multiples of '7', including God (35 or 7 x 5 times), earth (21 times), heavens (21 times), and "God saw that it was good" (7 times). There are parallels to the construction of the Tabernacle, since this process also lasted '7' days. There are also key correspondences between the two processes. As well as many of the Hebrew phrases being almost identical in both stories, some of the individual days also show similarities. For example, God created the sea on the third day; and in the construction of the Tabernacle, the bronze laver or molten 'sea' was built on the third day. Similarly, Moses stressed the importance of the Sabbath for Israel on the seventh day, just as Genesis tells us how God rested on the seventh day.

One may also be struck that Solomon's Temple took seven years to build (the number '7' is important here as a symbol: in religious books days, months, years and centuries are often less important than the number attributed). The seventh year is called a 'Sabbath'. The dedication took place during the seven-day Festival of Tabernacles, which fell in the seventh month of the Jewish

Figure 61- 'Transfiguration' by Cornelis Monsma

calendar. King Solomon's speech included seven petitions; and Solomon was instruction to build the Temple rather than David because Solomon was a man of peace, as his name *shlomoh* implies. These numbers were not selected at random, the repeatedly emphasize that fact that the Temple construction as viewed as a new creation, and therefore the completed Temple a 'microcosm' of the world, which in symbolic form, tried to recreate the Garden of Eden prior to the Fall, when all was perfect and God dwelt in the midst of the Garden, in Eden; just as He now dwelt in the *Sanctum Sanctorum*, hidden behind a veil decorated with pomegranates and cherubim.

How more tragic, then, that the next prevarication of man resulted in the same fate: the departure of God, the razing of the Temple and man expelled into exile once more.

However, the word 'microcosm' brings us to a second symbol of the Temple: that of perfect – or regenerated – man. The Kabbalah teaches us that God wished to see Himself face to face, to gaze upon His reflection. And so, He created Adam Kadmon in His image and likeness, and placed him in Eden. But man heeded the voices of the tempters, and believing himself as powerful as God attempted his own act of creation, but only resulted in enmiring himself in the very mud from which he was trying to create another being, and became covered with a layer or slime – or flesh. So perfect man is hidden beneath a coating of sin, and must learn to perfect himself in order to cast off this earthly coating, and reveal his true form, his Glorious Body, to rejoin with the Godhead. To do this he must recognize the Truth about himself.

In this Degree, this image is most powerfully put across by the fact that there are in fact *two* completions. During the procession, the Keystone is carried in and placed. This completes the physical structure of the Temple. The outer vehicle is finished. To emphasize this point, after the second procession the aprons are removed. In terms of the Creation, the body is now formed. Man exists, but he is still nothing more than an empty shell.

Now the *second* completion takes place. The Ark of the Covenant is brought in and 'safely seated.' God once again shows His approbation in air. At the Creation God breathed life into the inert dross by exhaling the breath of life into Adam. This time God's spirit, or Shekinah, descends from the heavens and fills the Temple, inflating it into life. Now I stress that this is a personal *exegesis* or interpretation drawn from the actual text:

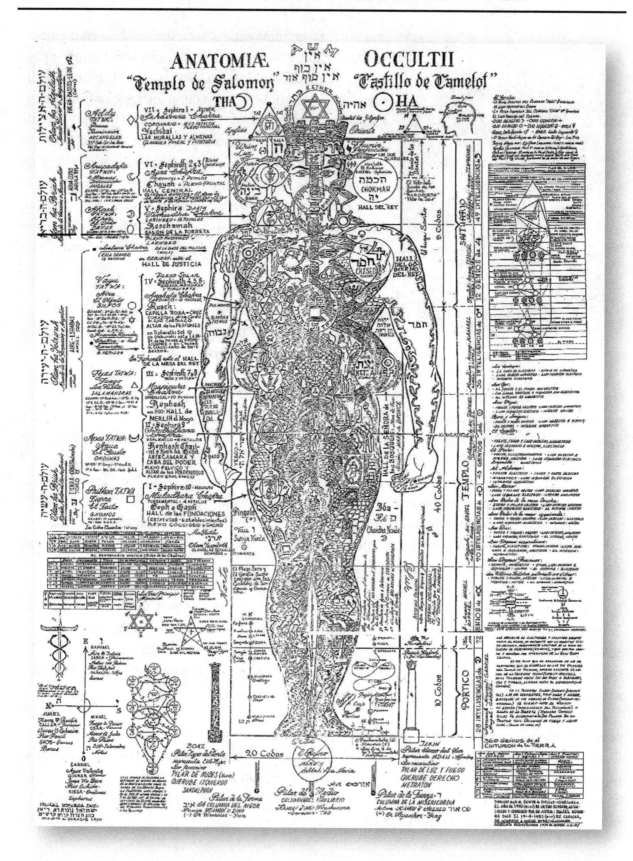

Figure 62 - A complex diagram equating Adam Kadmon to King Solomon's Temple and Camelot!

"Now when Solomon had made an end of praying, the fire came down from heaven, and consumed the burnt offering and the sacrifices; and the glory of the Lord filled the house. And the priests could not enter into the house of the Lord, because the glory of the Lord had filled the Lord's house." (2 Chronicles 7, verses 1 and 2).

My reading of this passage is that the fire came down to consume the sacrifices, but the Glory of the Lord is mentioned separately – and several times in the text which follows – suggesting it is something different, not fire. After all, if fire had filled the temple it would have melted all the gold and fused the precious stones, and immolated the priests and Levites! However, if we accepted that His Glory was found in the element of air, then this makes more sense. God's presence is frequently represented by fire if He is wrathful, but by air or wind if His approbation has been given to a project.

For me it is a powerful image to see God entertaining the masses in the outer Courtyard with impressive displays of pyrotechnics; while inside the Temple He manifests Himself in a mighty wind against which the priests and Levites have to brace themselves, and the curtains before the Ark are blown open and the incense swirls about the Sanctum Sanctorum, before the Shekinah finally comes to settle between the outstretched wings of the cherubim. And thus, God breathes life into the Temple.

But I stress again this is only one interpretation of the Biblical passage, and readers are encouraged to draw their own conclusions.

Finally, after the plethora of 'sevens' mentioned in the text, it almost comes as a relief to read 2 Chronicles 7 Verse 9:

"And in the eighth day they made a solemn assembly: for they kept the dedication of the altar seven days, and the feast seven days."

After the cycle of creation and the day of rest which had been spent in joyous celebration, we reach the number 'eight', the number of renewal and new beginnings. We see the tone of this eighth day is solemn following the joy of the previous week. For life goes on, and Day 1 of life with *God-With-Us* now begins. For us it is Day 1 of our spiritual rebirth, and the first day in a new journey along the Masonic path.

The First Temple was also seen as a symbol for Man, with the Holy of Holies his Head, or Spirit; the Holy Place his Heart, Soul or Chest; and the Outer Courts his Body, Abdomen or Genitalia (one might make a case for the Two Pillars being his legs). While not wishing to do more than mention this concept now, it is nevertheless important to realize that the Temple was seen, even when the narrative was originally being written, as far more than a simple tale about the erection of a lovely building. Even then it was seen as representing a microcosm of creation, and a microcosm of all that man should aspire to in order to perfect himself, in preparation for reunion with God.

Figure 63 - The Torah

In support of this, although tradition informs us that the five books of Moses, the Torah, were written by Moses himself, modern theologians date the writing of the Torah which exists today – which no doubt existed in oral, and perhaps written form for many centuries before this – as being during the period of exile in Babylon, when the priests, having no idea how long their exile would last, wished to ensure that their traditions, beliefs and regulations would not be lost to the new generations being born in Babylon with no link or knowledge of the land of their ancestors.

Esoteric Implications

There are many lessons to draw from this impressive and educational Degree. Many have been alluded to already. For the present, we will limit ourselves to one: the penalties of the Degrees.

Many comments have been made about the penalties, whether they were ever carried out (as the anti-Masons like to think); whether they should explicitly be said to be only symbolic; whether they should be omitted altogether as they have been, for example, in Ireland. However, this misses the point that the penalties are – just as the rest of the Rituals are – allegories which use powerful and visceral symbols to transmit important teachings.

Figure 64 - Count Cagliostro, founder of the Rite of Memphis

The road to the Royal Arch in the York Rite system really comprises *four* preceding Degrees, the Entered Apprentice, Fellowcraft, Master Mason and Most Excellent Master. The Mark Master and Past Master are really side Degrees, appended to the Fellowcraft and Master Mason Degree respectively. There are four *real* steps to the Degree of Royal Arch. We may speculate this was a process being introduced into the English System, too, particularly within the Antient rituals; but that the process broke down when politics intervened to crush their natural and organic development through the Act of Union in 1813.

The penalty of Most Excellent Master, when taken along with those of Entered Apprentice, Fellowcraft and Master Mason, cover the four ancient elements. Trial by element is a concept which goes back to the Ancient Mystery Schools, and is still practiced in some Masonic Rituals, including those of Memphis-Mizraïm, the Scottish Rite and Willermoz' Scottish Rectified Rite. It can also be witnessed in the biennial conferral of the Entered Apprentice Degree by Garibaldi Lodge No. 542 under the authority of the Grand Lodge of New York F. & A.M.

- In the Entered Apprentice Degree the tongue is removed and buried in **Water**.
- In the Fellowcraft Degree the heart and lungs are removed and left as prey to the vultures of the **Air**.
- In the Master Mason Degree the bowels are removed and burned to ashes (with **Fire**).
- In the Most Excellent Master Degree *all* the internal organs are removed (the 'vitals') and thrown on a dunghill (**Earth**).

This is a powerful Rosicrucian concept and reflects true spiritual alchemy. Writers from early alchemists to Carl Jung have written about the need to deconstruct the body in order to understand and balance its elements, in order to create a perfect abode for the spirit to enter. It appear that Freemasonry may have picked something up from the Rosicrucians, after all.

Figure 65 - The Four Classical Elements

MEM - Quiz #3

1   Did Thomas Smith Webb compose the Most Excellent Master Degree?
(a) Yes.
(b) No.
(c) Parts of it.
(d) Perhaps.

2   Where did Thomas Smith Webb most likely get his inspiration for his work on the Most Excellent Master Degree?
(a) St. Andrew's Royal Arch Lodge in Massachusetts.
(b) Temple Lodge in New York.
(c) Bon Accord Lodge in Scotland.
(d) None of the above.

3   Which General Grand High Priest had a major reputation as a supporter of the Capitular Rituals?
(a) Albert Gallatin Mackey?
(b) Dr. William Frederick Kuhn?
(c) Charles Gilman?
(d) All the above?

4   What period in Jewish history does the Most Excellent Master Degree cover?
(a) The laying of the cornerstone?
(b) The visit of the Queen of Sheba?
(c) The completion and dedication of the Temple?
(d) The destruction of the Temple?

5   Which Bible mentioned the word 'Giblim' in a footnote?
(a) King James Bible?
(b) Geneva Bible?
(c) American Standard Version Bible?
(d) World English Bible?

6   Who did Thomas Smith Webb know and work with?
(a) DeWitt Clinton and Ezra Ames.
(b) Ezra Ames only.
(c) DeWitt Clinton, Ezra Ames and Giles Fonda Yates.
(d) Giles Fonda Yates only.

7   With what is the Candidate tried upon entering the Lodge?
(a) Compasses.
(b) Gavel or Mallet.
(c) Chisel.
(d) Keystone.

8   How many circumambulations are there in the first part of the Degree?
(a) Three.
(b) Four.
(c) Six.
(d) Seven.

9   What is the grip of Most Excellent Master sometimes called?
(a) Excellent Master Grip.
(b) Cover Grip.
(c) Keystone Grip.
(d) Masking Grip.

10   Which stone is actually placed in the Ritual of Most Excellent Master?
(a) Cape-stone.
(b) Cornerstone.
(c) Copestone.
(d) Keystone.

11   What does the fire descending from heaven represent?
(a) The wrath of God.
(b) The Shekinah.
(c) Lightning.
(d) A Hollywood FX.

12   Who recites Psalm 122?
(a) King Solomon.
(b) The Chaplain.
(c) The Most Excellent Masters.
(d) King Solomon and Hiram King of Tyre.

13   What does 'that far distant country' refer to?
      (a) A foreign country.
      (b) Sleep.
      (c) Scotland.
      (d) Death.

14   Which of the four classical elements does the penalty of Most Excellent Master recall?
      (a) Earth.
      (b) Air.
      (c) Fire.
      (d) Water.

MEM Discussion Questions

1   What is your opinion of removing your aprons as part of this Degree? Do you think you should remove aprons in a Lodge, when we are taught always to be clothed in Lodge? Does it violate the Constitutions? Does the end (i.e. to teach a lesson) justify the means?

2   Do you think the Degree system would be as effective without the Most Excellent Master Degree? We know that it doesn't exist in England, for existence, as part of the Capitular experience. In your opinion, what does its presence add to the York Rite?

3   The text examined the symbolism of the Elements in the penalties associated with the Degrees in some depth. In the Third Degree, you were presented with a number of symbols, for example the Hourglass, the Beehive, the Anchor and the Ark, and were given some explanations of their meanings. Do you think that was all they might represent?

At the Completion of the Temple a large number of vessels and objects were carried up into the Temple. The Key ones, some of which we will again encounter in the Royal Arch Degree include the horned Altar of Holocausts (or Sacrifice), the Sea or Laver of Brass, the Seven-Branched Candelabra, the Altar of Incense, the Table of Shewbread (bearing twelve loaves of unleavened bread, and wine), and the Ark of the Covenant. Can you think of what any or all of these vessels and equipment might symbolize in this analogy?

4   Do you think the Most Excellent Master Degree was written merely to fill a gap in the narrative about the Temple, or do you think it was written with a higher purpose in mind?

Figure 66 - Engraving of the Dedication of the Temple, with the fire descending from Heaven

Holy Royal Arch Degree

Brief History

The history of the Royal Arch has been outlined in the Background and History of the Capitular Degrees at the beginning of this course. However, it is important to consider a few points specific to the origin of the Royal Arch Degree itself.

Figure 67 - The Great Seal of the Grand Lodge of New York clearly shows its Antient origins, and depicts the Royal Arch banner and motto

The origins of the Royal Arch are hard to determine. There appear to be two major movements. The first suggests that it was imported from Ireland by the Irish Masons living in England – especially around London – and was part of the reason that the Antients seceded from the Moderns, since the latter appeared not to want to work it. This, it is claimed, is why the Antients worked the Degree while the Moderns did not, and why Laurence Dermott called it the "very root, heart and marrow of Freemasonry." This does seem to run into trouble when we study the private correspondence of prominent Moderns, however, and we have already quoted James Heseltine, Grand Secretary of the Moderns from 1769 who wrote that "many of the Fraternity here belong to a Degree in Masonry…called the Royal Arch." So the Degree was by no means unknown to the Moderns, notwithstanding it was not 'officially' recognized until the Act of Union in 1813.

We mentioned briefly earlier, there is another view which suggests that, in fact, the Royal Arch not only existed prior to the Third Degree, but that the reason we do not see much mention of it until much later in historical terms is because there was no Royal Arch Degree originally – at least not called by that name – for it was the Installation Ritual of a Master. This becomes a problem, since if we cannot trace it by name, how are we to identify its origins? The answer is, we cannot. However, this does not prevent us from exercising our deductive skills in asking ourselves whether there are any hints of its existence prior to 1717.

Historically, the times leading up to the formation of the Premier Grand Lodge in 1717 were, to say the least, tumultuous! James I of England (VI of Scotland) had come to the throne in 1603, had given us the King James Bible, and was succeeded in 1625 by his son, Charles I. This unfortunate monarch was beheaded in 1649 following the battles with the Cromwellian forces in the civil war of England, and following this regicide, Cromwell ruled as king in all but name, imposing his dour Protestantism upon the English people until 1659.

Figure 68 - Satirical cartoon showing the Roundheads (Cromwellian forces) against the Cavaliers (forces of the Monarchy)

The restoration of the monarchy came in 1660, and Charles II ascended to the throne. Most of the English were sick and tired of the measures imposed by Cromwell and his supporters. Despite the present-day view of the English as being self-controlled and uptight, the opposite was true in those days, and England was known for ribald behavior and merrymaking. Under Cromwell, churchgoing had been compulsory; horse racing and cockfights banned, as were drunkenness and blasphemy. Plays, brothels and gambling houses were banned, and many ale houses closed. It was not long before the public decided they hated armies and Puritanism even more (which is why they came to the United States!).

Figure 69 - Bonnie Prince Charlie, the Young Pretender

Life was fun under Charles II, but when James II came to the throne in 1685, his attempt to reintroduce the Roman Catholic faith and to rein in the excesses of his father's reign met with strong opposition, and led to his fleeing the country (and therefore assumed to have abdicated) in 1688, being replaced by his elder Protestant daughter, Mary II, and her husband William III from Orange, a region of Holland. Their short reigns were followed by the equally short reign of their daughter, Mary, and by 1714 they were already casting around to find another successor, since it was clear that Parliament would not consider any progeny of James II, especially since his son had attempted to invade England thought Scotland in 1708, and again in 1715, the year after George I ascended the throne. His grandson, Bonnie Prince Charlie, or the Young Pretender, also organized an invasion via Scotland in 1745, which was unsuccessful, since he was defeated at the battle of Culloden, and that ended the Jacobite claims to the English throne. George I continued to rule until his death in 1727, during which time he never spoke a word of English.

The point we should draw from all this British history is the incredible state of flux England found itself in during that short period of time. It had gone from an apparently stable monarchy in 1649 through a period of hardship under a Commonwealth run by a virtual dictator (Cromwell) for a period of 10 years. This was followed by a self-indulgent 25 years under Charles II, during which time a great plague affected London in 1665, followed by the Great Fire which razed most of the center of London in 1666. Sir Christopher Wren and others

Figure 70 - The London Great Plague of 1665

were tasked with rebuilding the city in stone, and suddenly Masons from all over England were invited to come to London to help with the rebuilding, being offered Freedom of the City[2] by the Crown after seven years of labor. Now, many churches and major buildings had Lodges attached,

Figure 71 - The London Great Fire of 1666

either to maintain the buildings (one may see this tradition continued today at the cathedral of St. John the Divine in New York City) or to rebuild them following the Great Fire of London. It is a fact that Sir Christopher Wren belonged to the Lodge attached to St. Paul's Churchyard. In 1689 the English saw their King depart from England and a new Protestant couple come from Holland to rule them. But at least Mary was of the bloodline of James II. By 1714 Anne was dead and now they took a

---

[2] ***Freedom of the City*** was an honor bestowed upon servants or serfs in olden times for services rendered to the Monarch, and later to Parliament or to the City Council, which entailed them being released from bondage and allowed to own property, to trade in their own name, and in some instances, the right to vote. Nowadays it is a largely ceremonial ritual, conferred upon visiting dignitaries or as recognition for long service.

German prince (in fact Hanoverian, since what is now Germany was a collection of Electorates or local Princes at the time) to be their King. Within a year they were being attacked by Jacobite forces, which were repelled, and within two more years the Premier Grand Lodge was being established.

Figure 70 - King George I

To the average English native, it must have seemed like the end of the world. For most of them little of consequence had happened on English soil since the Wars of the Roses some two hundred years earlier, and most famous battles had been fought overseas in mainland Europe. But now their land had seen tyrants rule, kings beheaded, plagues, conflagrations, exiles, monarchs seemingly invading from Holland and Germany, all in the space of a few years. Each change in government brought new foes, and those who were one's friends, employers or work colleagues could be the 'enemy' the following year.

The atmosphere at that time was perhaps not unlike the McCarthy period in America, where everyone in this case was looking at their neighbor, wondering if they were secretly harboring sympathies for the exiled Jacobite Royal family! No wonder the new Grand Lodge felt it necessary both to show clear loyalty for the King (while their antecedents were most likely to have been supporters of the house of Stuart), and divest themselves of any indication that they might have had prior connections to earlier royal dynasties. For one thing, it was important that their history began then, in 1717, after the attempted revolutions.

Imagine being born into a wealthy family in London, say in 1640, under an apparently stable monarchy. You saw your monarch executed when you were 9 years old, and lived the next 10 years of your life in fear of persecution as being a Cavalier (we all remember the famous painting 'And when did you last see your father' by William Frederick Yeames, portraying the young boy standing before his Roundhead inquisitors). At 19 the monarchy is restored and life seems to be good! And yet within five years your very life is being threatened with a deadly plague, and a year later to you see your beloved city burn to the ground. Fortunately, being of wealthy stock you spent most of 1665 on the country estate, and in 1666 you have returned to a

Figure 71- Detail of Yeames' painting "And when did you last see your father?"

stone mansion on the outskirts of London City. During this period, you enjoy the blessing of nearly twenty peaceful and entertaining years, and then, when you turn 49 the King departs and you see a succession of three foreign monarchs within the space of a few years, and throughout this time you are under suspicion of being a possible Jacobite sympathizer. You have to watch everything you say and do, the company you keep, where you travel, how you live. There are spies everywhere. And every time the Pretenders attempt to invade England the hysteria breaks out again. Finally, in 1715, when you turn the great old age of 65, you find yourself one final time having to prove

your loyalty. You had been a Freemason for many years, and it mattered not that you spoke not at all about politics in Lodge: despite the wonderful times you spent, and the deep philosophical discussions you enjoyed, you were aware that your friends in Lodge comprised both Protestants and Catholics, and this was a factor which drove the need to tile the meetings and keep your conversations secret. Finally, in your winter years, you see the Craft you so enjoyed as a haven from all the nonsense going on around you during your life

Figure 72 - Early London Table Lodge

transformed into a shadow of its earlier self, a body determined to seek patronage from the incumbent royal family, and prove its loyalty to a little know minor German prince. Part of this process include pretending you didn't exist prior to this time; and...by abandoning some of the most beautiful teachings of Freemasonry.

Of course, this image is fictitious; but it is intended to show some of the currents behind why the new Grand Lodge might have decided to invent a new ritual – the Third Degree – which records indicate strongly was not created until the mid-1720s; and deemphasize some of the colorful ritual associated with earlier times.

A close study of the Third Degree clearly shows that it is incomplete. It ends with the conferral of a substitute word and substitute actions, and given that the whole of Freemasonry emphasizes the importance of the numbers three, and the fact that this number features so heavily in its symbolism, it makes almost no sense that the crowning moment of the Master Mason Degree should involve two men grappling as if seeking to find comfort in one another while they whisper a seemingly meaningless word into each other's ear. Once we arrive at the Royal Arch Degree we see the importance of the number three restored, as well as the word; and instead of groping almost blindly at one another, three men now come together in an elegant manner to exchange what is no longer a meaningless word, but perhaps the most important word in Western history. The first thought that many new Masons have when they have completed the Third Degree is: when do I get the *real* word?

There are two main hypotheses concerning the Royal Arch Degree. Either it was the completion of the earlier Master Mason Degree; or it was an Installed Master Degree, which a Fellowcraft elected to govern a Lodge received in order to qualify him for the position, when there was only one Master Mason – the Mason who ruled his Lodge.

Now, the main objections point to the fact that it is well-known the Third Degree did not come into existence until the mid-1720s. Surely, then, if the Third Degree didn't exist prior to that time, the Royal Arch could not have existed either? However, an alternative explanation could be that what the Grand Lodge was attempting to do was to replace the *existing* Third Degree.

Now, the completely fictitious story of Hiram's death was introduced (nowhere is it mentioned in the Bible) and a new word and signs substituted to create a completely new Degree. To do this the old Degree, which contained a straightforward story of the Temple's completion and the conferral of the True Master's Word had to be dropped. This new Third Degree had to be presented as though it was 'new' and was not replacing anything which had come before. Consider the

Figure 73 - Mount Horeb

important Questions which are currently asked at the opening of all Festive Boards in England, which indicate there were Three Grand Lodges, the first being the Holy Lodge at the foot of Mount Horeb, the Second or Sacred Lodge held on Mount Moriah by King Solomon, and the Third or Royal Lodge held in Jerusalem, and presided over by Zerubbabel (we shall see this in more detail later). There is every evidence from its separation from the rest of the ritual and from the fact that it is in form of a catechism – an early device – that it may be of great antiquity. If so, and if the Royal Arch was based on the story of Zerubbabel, it would make sense for the 'new' Third Degree to be based upon the story of the Second Grand Lodge, which had been formed for the purpose of building King Solomon's Temple. By homing in on an earlier Biblical event perhaps the intention was to make the 'new' Degree appear older; just as the Antients who formed in opposition to the practices of the Premier Grand Lodge took that title to give the impression that they had been around longer (and perhaps, if the Royal Arch was the senior Degree, in principle they had)?

Further, Gerhard Schott's huge set of King Solomon's Temple, designed for Christian Hienrich Postel's opera in Hamburg about the destruction of the Temple, had been displayed in a number of European cities following the production. One of these was London, where it was on display for a number of years, where it no doubt caught the attention of Freemasons of the time. An engraving of the design also became the most common depiction of Solomon's Temple in Bibles printed in England for nearly 100 years, and also featured hanging on the wall in numerous

Masonic engravings of the mid- to late 1700s. With this double influence of a physical representation of the Temple exhibited in London, and the Royal Arch catechism, we have two possible sources of the 'new', or what a number of contemporaries called the 'casual' Master Mason Degree.

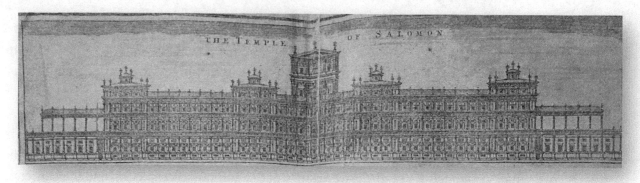

Figure 74 - Engraving of Solomon's Temple from a 1767 Baskett Bible

Figure 75 - Early engraving of a meeting in London - note the image on the wall is of Schott's Solomonic Temple

So we can conclude that there was possibly a movement around the time that the Grand Lodge was established in 1717 to create a Third Degree which was not associated with the previous roots, and indeed within a handful of years this new society was attracting both aristocracy and even members of the (new) Royal family. It is therefore no surprise that a number of contemporary Freemasons who lived in and around London, but whose roots were decidedly more pro-Stuart –

especially those of Irish decent, who remembered their country's Masonry – should consider the adoption of a new Degree, at the expense of one they held dear, one of the major reasons they decided to secede and form their own, Antient, Grand Lodge.

The Royal Arch in the United States

As we have seen, much of this was either unknown or a matter of indifference to American Freemasons. We have seen that the first global reference to a Royal Arch Meeting was in Fredericksburg, VA in December 1753. We also know that many Lodges were established by Antient Charters or by traveling military groups which established Lodges which would have practiced the Antient Degrees. To this we can add those who had traveled to Europe, to England, France, Spain, Germany, Ireland and Scotland, for pleasure or trade, and either joined Lodges there or visited Lodges having been initiated in the colonies; and who brought back their experiences of visiting those Lodges and Chapters. Finally, we know that a number of groups were practicing Royal Arch rituals prior to the establishment of the General Grand Chapter in 1797 and the codification of the rituals by Thomas Smith Webb. For example, there is evidence that Independent Royal Arch Lodge, No. 2, in New York City was practicing a form of Royal Arch Ritual early on; as well as Ancient Chapter No. 1, formerly Old Chapter, whose origin tradition fixes to be 1763, since its early records were lost through fire. 'Old Chapter' was old enough to refuse immediate admission to the Grand Chapter of New York when it formed in March 1798, and had issued its *own* Charters to Chapters in New York, New Jersey and Connecticut *prior* to that date. The new Grand Chapter held it in sufficiently high regard to keep the number '1' open until such time as it decided to join eight years later, in 1806.

We are therefore fortunate that our roots are heavily in the Antient tradition, since the Royal Arch was largely lost and forgotten by the Moderns by then, while the tradition of preserving the True Word was very much alive in the former Grand Body and its missionaries, the military Lodges.

Overview of the Degree

The Degree is quite long and complex. Before we examine each section in detail it might be useful to have a general overview of the Royal Arch Degree:

A. The Candidates receive some instruction on the History of the Degree prior to entering the Chapter.
B. The Candidates are prepared and enter the Lodge 'under a Living Arch'.
C. The Candidates pray, then rise and circumambulate, when they are challenged by the Captain of the Host.

D. The Candidates take their Obligation at the West Altar.

E. The Candidate perform six more circumambulations, during which they see the burning bush, learn the password, and are taken to the first (closed) veil.

F. The Candidates pass each of the veils, with the Principal Sojourner answering the challenges on their behalf.

G. On gaining access to the High Council the Candidates, now Sojourners as they wish to sojourn with their fellow Israelites, are armed with a crow, pickaxe and spade, and sent to clear the rubbish.

H. They make three important discoveries: a keystone, three squares, and the Ark of the Covenant. These are discovered buried in a vault, and brought to the light of day.

I. The Sojourners bring their discoveries to the High Council.

J. Inside the Ark the High Council find the Book of the Law, Pot of Manna and Aaron's Rod, as well as a scroll.

K. Reading the scroll and deciphering the strange writing in the Masonic Alphabet around the Ark, the High Council rediscovers the Lost Master's Word and the Great And Sacred Name.

L. As a reward the secrets of the Degree are conferred upon the Sojourners and the method of forming the Living Arch demonstrated.

M. Several Instructional Lectures on the Apron, the History, the Masonic Alphabet and the Banner are given.

N. The Ceremony concludes with an Address and the Charge.

Furniture and Dress

Figure 76 - York Rite Royal Arch Apron

Companions wear white aprons bordered with red, with a Triple Tau emblem in red upon the flap of the apron. We are told in the opening that the color red is the appropriate color of Royal Arch Masons, since it symbolizes "that fervency and zeal which should even actuate royal Arch Masons." Incidentally, you will sometimes see Royal Arch Masons signing their letters with **WFZ**, meaning 'with fervency and zeal'; just as many Blue Lodge Masons sign off with **S&F**, or 'sincerely and fraternally'.

The Officers up to the Captain of the Host also wear swords, and whenever interacting with a senior Officer will draw their sword and salute that officer. The only exception is the Principal Sojourner, and this is more on account of the fact that he carries a staff, which reminds us of the staff carried by Moses.

Figure 77 - Beating the Bounds, an ancient church ceremony where the bounds of the parish are indicated by willow sticks carried by the priest and church wardens, to teach the children – sometimes forcibly – the edges of their parish

There is a suggestion that the staff is also descended from early days in operative Lodges, where the rulers of the Lodge carried wands or staves to indicate their status. This practice may also be seen in churches, where the church wardens traditionally carry rods. Similarly, Black Rod and White Rod are officers in the Houses of Parliament in England; and Marshalls and other commissioned officers carry wands in the armed forces. It is believed that, as the line of Officers expanded within Lodges, and the lesser duties of the senior officers were delegated to the Deacons, they now carry the staves to indicate their delegated powers. Vestiges of these staves may also be seen in those carrying the four banners under the control of the Royal Arch Captain and three Masters of the Veils.

The Triangular Altar normally resides in the East of the Chapter Room, and bears the Holy Bible. Each of the four Degrees has a prescribed passage to which the Bible must be opened for each Degree; and the Square and Compasses are in their usual position when the Chapter is opened. The four passages used are:

- **Mark Master Degree** (blue ribbon) – **Matthew Chapter 20**: The first 15 verses tell the story of the man who hired laborers to work in his vineyard, thee story read by the Right Worshipful Master during the Closing of the Degree.

- **Virtual Past Master Degree** (purple ribbon) – **Ecclesiastes Chapter 12**: This is the passage also used during the Obligation of a Master-elect in a regular Blue Lodge.

- **Most Excellent Master Degree** (red ribbon) – **2 Chronicles 6**: This is the passage describing King Solomon's dedication of the Temple at Jerusalem.

- **Holy Royal Arch Degree** & Regular Communications (white ribbon) – **Ezra Chapter 1**: This contains the Proclamation of King Cyrus and the list of the treasures taken from the First Temple which the Jews carried back with them.

In addition to the banners of the Royal Arch Captain and the Masters of the Veils, each Chapter should have its own Chapter banner. The Royal Arch Banner or Standard is effectively that of the Antient Grand Lodge of England, establish in 1751.In its center it is composed of the banners of the four tribes Judah, Reuben, Ephraim and Dan, surmounted by the Ark of the Covenant, and flanked by two Cherubim. The Antients motto is often seen on them as well, which is Holiness To The Lord (originally in Hebrew on the Antient's banner). The Banner will normally also bear the name and number of the Chapter.

The other furnishings are covered in the appropriate passage in the following sections.

Figure 78 - Banner of Oxford Chapter In New York. Note the similarity with the Grand Lodge of New York Great Seal

Opening & Closing

Regardless of which of the four Capitular Degrees is being worked, the Chapter will always open on the Holy Royal Arch Degree. If necessary, the Lodge will then be lowered to be appropriate Degree. When a Degree other than the Holy Royal Arch is being worked, care should be taken to remove those elements which are specific to that Degree (the four Banners, the Veils, the Ark, the Candelabra, etc.).

When a Chapter is about to open, there are nine essential Officers present. These are the High Priest, King, Scribe, the Captain of the Host, Principal Sojourner, Royal Arch Captain, and the Three Masters of the Veils.

In the East is the High Priest who presides, with the King to his right and Scribe to his left. These three compose the High Council. The Treasurer and Secretary occupy their usual stations. The Captain of the Host occupies the seat used by the Senior Deacon in Blue Lodge, and the Principal Sojourner that of the Marshall. Down the South side of the Chapter are four seats, occupied from East to West by the Royal Arch Captain, Master of the Third Veil, Master of the Second Veil, and Master of the First Veil. The Sentinel is outside, fulfilling the role of Tiler.

Behind the Royal Arch Captain is the white banner upon a stave. Behind the Master of the Third Veil is the Red banner; behind the Master of the Second Veil the purple banner; and behind the Master of the first Veil the blue banner. In the East is the triangular altar, bearing the Holy Bible.

The Chapter Opening largely follows the order of opening a Blue Lodge. After a purging of the Chapter, the Sentinel is informed the Chapter is about to open and guards the Outer Door. Since the Junior Officers are armed, the Royal Arch Captain is saluted by the Veils as he passes to interact with the Sentinel, and again on his return. The Captain of the Host is then challenged in a catechism with the High Priest, and proceeds to the rehearsal of the Officers' duties. These duties are a summary of those given at length during the Holy Royal Arch Degree. Again, each Officer steps forward and salutes with his sword when questioned.

At this point the Officers lead a procession of all the Companions around the Chapter, and end up forming a circle about the Triangular Altar, joining hands, right arm

Figure 79 - Triangular Altar

over left, to form a Chain of Fraternal Union. They are then joined by the High Council and a prayer offered. Following the prayer, they bounce (the archaic word is 'balance') their arms three times and break the Chain.

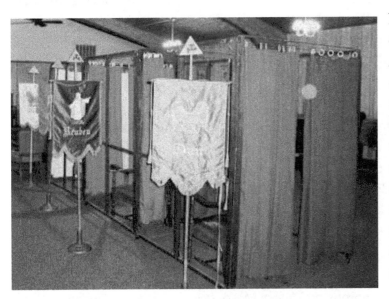

Figure 80 - Hillsboro Chapter, Illinois (ram-il.org/chapters/chapters-furnishings)

Note how the words used during the opening are almost like a mantra. Also, while the lines don't completely rhyme (except 'three' and 'agree') the meter is very poetic, and reminds us of early Degrees which used to communicate in rhyming verse, such as the Royal Order of Scotland. This suggests this formula, whose style does not really fit exactly with the rest of the Opening Ceremony, may be very old.

Now they form in groups of three to 'raise the Royal Arch'. Here we realize the Royal Arch is not just a reference to the arch of masonry held in place by the keystone in the East. The Royal Arch is a living Arch, made up of living stones. The threes form a triangle with their feet, and two triangles with their left and right hands, again emphasizing the idea of 'three times three'. In this position, they then repeat the High Priest's words. It is interesting to note that, traditionally, those forming the Royal Arches do not look directly at each other, but turn their heads to the left and look over their left shoulder. While it is not certain where this tradition comes from, it is most likely simply because oral hygiene wasn't very good two or three hundred years ago, and this was to spare the other two Companions from the stench of acute halitosis!

Once the word is exchanged in syllables three times, the Royal Arches are broken and the High Priest instructs the Captain of the Host to have the Bible opened and the Sentinel informed that the Chapter is open. He instructs the Principal Sojourner to open the bible and the Royal Arch Captain to inform the Sentinel. Note that it is appropriate of the Principal Sojourner to open the Bible, since in the Royal Arch Degree he is both the Candidates' guide, and also the expounder of biblical passages during their travels. Similarly, as the guardian of the fourth and final veil and therefore responsible for protecting the High Council, it is appropriate that the Royal Arch Captain also defends the Outer Door.

Once the Chapter is opened, the Captain of the Host and Royal Arch Captain process to the West of the Chapter, where the Captain of the host occupies the Senior Warden's chair and the Royal Arch Captain the Junior Deacon's Chair (this is why the Royal Arch Captain is the only Officer to interact directly with the Sentinel). If there is an alarm at the Outer Door, the Royal Arch Captain brings it to the attention of the Captain of the Host, who reports it to the High Priest. The High Priest's instructions are communicated to the Captain of the Host, who communicates them to the Royal Arch Captain. Note that, unlike Blue Lodge, there is no direct communication between the Presiding Officer and the Royal Arch Captain. This is similar to the point in the opening of Lodge when the Worshipful Master communicated his intention to open the Lodge to the Senior Warden, and he to the Junior Warden.

When the Chapter is to close the Captain of the Host and Royal Arch Captain process back to their opening positions, and the Chapter is closed following the short form closing ritual. This was not always the case. Indeed, the Closing ritual of Ancient Chapter No. 1 which uses an old form, is more like the Closing of a Blue Lodge in that almost the entire Opening ritual apart from the purging is repeated.

Preparation of Candidates

The Candidates are clothed with white aprons as Master Masons, and also with sandals on both feet. They wear hoodwinks and a cabletow seven times round their waist.

They are Master Masons since they will now receive the true word and become Companions, which is the perfected state of a Mason. He is more than a Brother, which suggests a blood tie of obligation: he is now a Companion, a fellow traveler on the great journey of life, and his Obligations extend far further than mere family: now the entire human family has become his kin, and he labors for all mankind. There is a saying among those who follow the path of Transcendental Meditation (TM), that if only a small percentage of people, a number as little as 5%, practice TM, there would be no war, since the work of those few would affect all humanity. In a way, we are being asked to practice our tenets, and by our adherence to our values amongst our fellow man we are given the ability to leverage a change which would vastly supersede our numbers.

As we will see, the removing of shoes and putting on sandals is integral to the Degree ceremonies, and the cable tow in this instance refers to an event rather more powerful in symbolism to its use in prior Degrees. We are told that the High Priest entered the presence of the Lord but once a year, when he uttered the Sacred Name of God in order to reestablish the link between heaven and earth.

His garment was fringed will small bells, and a rope was tied around him the end leading out of the Holy of Holies, and held by the Kohenim or Levites. He uttered the Name while the priests and people made a great noise. However, this was a most dangerous operation, and if something went wrong – and the implication was that if the High Priest was in some way impure, or mispronounced the Name of God – his dead body could be pulled from the Holy of Holies by aid of the rope.

In Blue Lodge English Freemasonry, there is a line which effectively states that if the Candidate had attempted to escape the Lodge

Figure 81 - Moses commanded to take off his sandals before the Burning Bush

he would have been accomplice to his own death by strangulation, and in a way the cabletow therefore is a reflection of this binding to obligation, and the serious consequences to a person who does not behave according to his vow.

Two Altars

In the Degree of Holy Royal Arch we find two altars: one in the East, and one in the West. The one in the East is the regular triangular Altar which normally doubles as the Altar of Incense.

However, in some instances – for example the Dedication or Rededication of a Chapter – the ritual calls for three altars: a Western one, the familiar Eastern triangular one, to which the Holy Bible is carried and deposited, and a third Altar of Incense, which is traditionally a white double cube approximately following the description in Exodus.

Why the Eastern Altar should be triangular (which is unique to the United States: in almost all other countries it is a double cubical white altar) is a matter for debate. The most likely explanation is more prosaic than symbolic. It was probable that, at some point, it was decided to have a three-sided altar to emphasize the number three, and to distinguish the paraphernalia used in the Holy Royal Arch from that used in a Lodge Room.

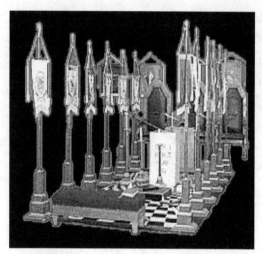

Figure 82 - In the English Domatic Ritual the Royal Arch Altar is a white double cube

The Obligation is taken facing West. Unusually it is not administered by the High Priest, but by the Captain of the Host, which in a Lodge analogy would be like being Obligated by the Marshall! Why is this? We must remember that Officers of a Lodge or Chapter often take on multiple roles, just as the Worshipful Master becomes King Solomon at certain points of Blue Masonry. In this instance, the Western part of the room represents Babylon, and the Captain of the Host is King Cyrus, while the Council represent Jeshua, Zerubbabel and Haggai, the High Priest, King and Prophet or Scribe. Following the Obligation, the Candidates will start to travel towards the light, or East in a Chapter Room, and towards Jerusalem.

Now, the Temple of Solomon was laid out so that one entered the outer courts in the East and progressed West towards the Holy of Holies. While the key passages in II Chronicles and I Kings do not explicitly tell us the Temple's orientation, we find it mentioned in Ezekiel 8:16: "And he brought me into the inner court of the Lord's house, and, behold, at the door of the temple of the Lord, between the porch and the altar, were about five and twenty men, with their backs toward the temple of the Lord, and their faces toward the east; and they worshipped the sun toward the east." What this is saying is that those men in the Temple had their backs to the Holy Place, and were facing the East to worship the rising sun. In other words, they were committing idolatry. Therefore, the entrance to the Holy Place must have been in the West.

This means the priests or Levites, who were the only ones permitted to enter to Holy Place, would return from the place which only they were permitted to enter, in order to instruct and educate the common people. This movement from the profane world in the East to the Holy Place in the West is exemplified in the story of the return from exile. Having been taken from their homeland to the foreign and alien city of Babylon, whose name means 'confused' in Hebrew, the exiles traveled West towards Jerusalem, which means 'foundation', or 'city of peace' in Hebrew. Symbolically, therefore, the people move from a lower plane (country) of profanity and confusion to a higher plane (country) of peace and contentment, and closeness to God. The symbolism of the Order of the Red Cross in the Templar Orders, for those who are considering continuing the York Rite journey, expresses this transition from one state to another even more forcibly.

This does raise one odd point regarding our Lodges and Chapters. Although they are set up for us to move from West to East in search of light, more light, further light, in fact the original journey from the outer court of the Temple, or the allegorical journey from Babylon to Jerusalem, both involved traveling from East to West!

Why is this?

Well, this may well be a situation where certain symbolism *trumps* other symbolism.

We are almost hard-wired to know the sun rises in the East. Symbolically the link between physical light and symbolic Light has been made is just about every civilization on the face of the earth. This is a strong symbol. Similarly, the orientation of all synagogues, mosques and churches towards the East – meaning towards Jerusalem – has been the practice for many centuries. Remember that the 'known world' was West of the Middle East for most of this period; also, Moslem tradition states that for the first thirteen years of Islam, mosques or prayer meetings were oriented towards Jerusalem, before Mohammad received a message from God to re-orientate towards Mecca.

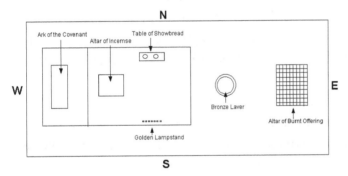

Figure 83 - Simplified Temple layout showing the entrance in the East and the Holy of Holies in the West (www.christian-restoration.com/fmasonry/temple.htm)

This brings us to one of the many bizarre accusations leveled against Freemasonry by people who have either too much time on their hands, see a conspiracy under every bed, or who are adept at misreading the Volume of the Sacred Law. It was mentioned above that Ezekiel criticized those who turned East to worship the sun. The point being made in the passage to any reasonable reader is that they were turning their backs on the place where God dwelt in order to worship a pagan concept of God. Since Jerusalem was considered an *omphalos* or navel of the world where the realms of heaven and earth met, where Adam had been formed and where Abraham had been called to sacrifice his son, it was less important which way the Temple was oriented, and indeed the first Temple was probably built along the most expedient axis given the hilly nature of the region. To give an example from one such site: "God's instructions were that His Tabernacle faced WEST - contrary to the pagan temples which all faced the sun in the east. As Masons face east toward the 'worshipful master' they face the symbol of the sun."

This is a curious claim on two counts.

Firstly, there is no explicit mention in Chronicles or Kings that God determined the orientation of the Temple. Secondly, one has to assume these people have curiously oriented places of worship, since as we just noted, every church, synagogue (and formerly mosque) was oriented to *Jerusalem*, towards the East in Europe and the Americas, as they have for upwards of two thousand years or more, towards that point where God first communicated with man. Perhaps these anti-Masons face the West and the setting sun when they pray, which is of course their right in a country which allows both freedom of religion and freedom of expression.

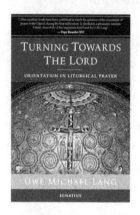

Figure 84 - A book which examines the orientation of believers when praying

From a Christian point of view, for example, Bishop Edward Slattery said: "... we find that the priest and the people faced in the same direction, usually toward the east, in the expectation that when Christ returns, He will return "from the east." At Mass, the Church keeps vigil, waiting for that return. This single position is called *ad orientem*, which simply means "toward the east." In *Turning Towards The Lord*, Lang says: "Despite all the variations in practice that have taken place far into the second millennium, one thing has remained clear for the whole of Christendom: praying towards the East is a tradition that goes back to the beginning.", and further: "Modern man has little understanding of this "orientation." Judaism and Islam, now as in the past, take it for granted that we should pray towards the central place of revelation, to the God who has revealed himself to us, in the manner and in the place in which he revealed himself."

Returning to the Royal Arch Degree, we note that later in this ritual the High Priest instructs the Sojourners that: "some more of the rubble be removed from the eastern part of the ruins", and it is there that they discover the Ark of the Covenant, which should properly be found in the Western part of the ruins.

So our religious experiences and our physical experiences tell us to seek light in the East. The fact that our Masonic experience runs contrary to this is probably secondary, and it simply made no sense to our forefather to build Masonic Temples which faced West rather than East. And there it is. Probably as simple as that!

Again, consider again the layout of the Temple. The entrance was in the East, and you traveled West to the Holy of Holies. While the physical sun rose in the East, true knowledge was to be sought at the place of the setting sun, which is where you also sought the body of Hiram Abif. "You cannot see my face, for no man may see me and live", said God (Exodus 33:20). To gaze upon pure, perfect, undiluted Truth we must ourselves pass beyond the veil of life. This profound Masonic teaching we will return to later. In the allegory of the Temple, we travel from East to West in fact, through the two columns, into the Middle Chamber, into the Holy Place, where we receive a substitute for Truth, being barred from the Veil(s) which separate us from the Holy of

Holies. Finally, in the Royal Arch Degree we pass through the veil and into the Divine Presence, whose very gaze strikes us dead. But we have a secret: as Companions we know His Name. "And the Truth shall set you free" (John 8:32).

Much food for thought.

A Living Arch

When the Candidate first enters the Lodge Room, he stands, blindfolded, between the two Columns of Boaz and Jachin which in some traditions represent the two columns of the Tree of Life, Severity and Mercy. Standing between them he represents the Middle Pillar, sometimes called Balance, Equilibrium or Mildness. It is this middle path to Truth which will occupy a lifetime of study and application for the serious Mason. For now he stands in the very place he will seek to return, but for now hoodwinked, and unaware where he stands.

Now, in a similar manner, the two has become three, duality divine, the opposing forces of the two pillars reconciled by the addition of the arch, the third force which holds the other two in balance. Once again, the Candidates will pass this way hoodwinked, unable to see that which will be revealed to him

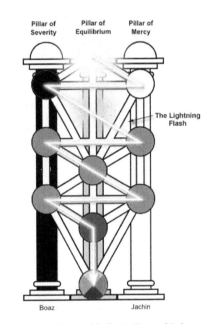

Figure 85 - The Kabbalistic Tree of Life, showing the Pillars of Boaz and Jachin, or Severity and Mercy

– indeed in which they themselves will participate – at the end of the ceremonies. As they enter the room the three Masters of the Veils form the Living Arch, and the three Candidates are told to "Stoop low, my Brothers, stoop low. He that humblest himself shall be exalted." The Candidates pass that way in single file, for they have not yet learned the Truth which will bind them together into a Living Arch themselves.

Figure 86 - The Arch resting upon the two Pillars

This is from the parable given in Luke Chapter 14, from which this quote comes. This reminds us that, although we are about to become Companions through a ceremony called Exaltation, we should remember that we should not allow this privilege or honor go to our heads. We may become more knowledgeable than our Brothers, but this does not make us any better than them: it simply means we may be half a step before them on the road to knowledge, and that it is our duty to help them to come to the same knowledge we now possess.

If you visit the Church of the Nativity in Manger Square, Bethlehem, you will find you have to "stoop low": in order to enter it. The entrance was lowered centuries ago to its present height of less than four feet in order to make it easier to secure against invaders, and now it is a salutary reminder to all who visit it that they should humble themselves before God.

The *Graham Manuscript*, comprising two scraps of paper dating to around 1726 (though it could be older given the odd spelling used), contain a reference to Bezaleel, about whom is said:

"the two younger brothers of the fforesaid king Alboyin desired
"for to be instructed by him his noble asiance by which he wrought
"to which he agreed conditionally they were not to discover it without
"another to themselves to make a trible voice"

(Transcribed by R∴W∴ Gary L. Heinmiller)

The reference to their needing three to make a 'trible voice' refers to the manner in which the True Word is communicated – a fact not covered at all in the present-day Master Masons Degree. All we are informed is that

Figure 87 – 'Stoop low' - Entrance to the Basilica of the Nativity, Bethlehem

two alone cannot complete the Word. Later the Candidates will learn how to give this Word "over a Triangle and under a Living Arch."

"I will Bring the Blind…"

The words of the Principal Sojourner are taken from Isaiah, and include Chapter 42 verse 16 and Chapter 40, verse 31.

In this Degree, the Principal Sojourner, takes the Blue Lodge role of Senior Deacon, acting as both guide and intermediary for the Candidate, answering when challenged on his behalf. In the Ancient Mysteries, this role was assumed by a person called the 'Psychopomp', where it was a guide from the land of the living to the dead (although that would also make sense in the Royal Arch Degree), but here it is used in the Jungian sense of being a mediator between the conscious and unconscious worlds. At the very basic level the Principal Sojourner leads a 'blind' Candidate and provides the appropriate passwords to gain access from one level to another.

Figure 88 - Anubis as Psychopomp, leading the deceased on his journey

He makes darkness light, which is most appropriate for a Mason seeking Light; and provides the very same encouragement which Isaiah did in his book of prophecy.

Isaiah lived and wrote during the period of Assyrian expansion and the decline of Judah. While Judah survived the threats from Assyria, Isaiah prophesied that Judah's sin would deliver her to Babylon. However, he also said that God would deliver a repentant people from Babylon just as he rescued them from Egypt. This is why these most appropriate passages are used at this time. Note that they immediately follow the opening prayer, which mentions that God appeared to Moses "in a flame of fire out of burning bush", thereby cementing together the two key themes of this Degree.

The Story of Moses

Figure 89 - A wonderfully anachronistic image called 'The Exposition of Moses' by Poussin of 'Et In Arcadia Ego' fame to those who have read the extravagant theories about Rennes-le-Chateau and the Prieurie de Sion. Note the mock medieval castle in the background

It is useful to remind ourselves briefly of the times in which Moses lived. Although Joseph had held a very high rank in Egypt, causing many Israelites to remain in that land, we are told that their race grew quickly in relation to the Egyptians, and after Joseph's death, the good that Joseph had done was quickly forgotten by later pharaohs in light of the high numbers of Israelites living under their rule. Concerned that they might take sides against Egypt in a future war, the Pharaoh enlisted them as slaves, and even demanded that any male child should be drowned at birth. Moses escaped this fate by being hidden from the guards, and then placed in an ark and hidden among the bulrushes. He was found by a daughter of the pharaoh and raised as her own.

When he was a young adult he saw Israelites being treated badly by an Egyptian guard and killed one, fleeing from the land to Midian, where he tended the flocks of Jethro, the father of his new bride Zipporah. It was while he was tending the sheep on Mount Horeb that God came to him in a burning bush, and told him to remove his shoes, since the place he stood was Holy ground.

Figure 90 - Byzantine mosaic of Moses and the Burning Bush - note the removal of his sandals

This was indeed a 'calling', for God called to Moses by name, and he answered: "Here am I." Here God tells him that He will deliver his people out of bondage in Egypt and take them to "a land flowing with milk and honey." He charges Moses with going to the new pharaoh – for his adoptive father had now died – and demand their release. But first Moses must convince the Israelites to follow him, and asks God his name. "I Am That I Am" is my name. However, His name is also given as Jahweh (or Jehovah), which is often substituted in the Bible for Adonaï, or The Lord, since Jews consider it blasphemous to utter the name of God, as that was originally reserved strictly to the High Priest, and only then once a year.

When Moses asks Him how he will convince the Israelites that he was indeed sent by God, he is given the three signs used during the Passing of the Veils to give them: the rod which becomes a serpent, the hand which becomes leprous, and the water which becomes blood. Moses also laments the fact that he is not gifted with eloquent speech, and God tells him to enlist Aaron his brother to speak on his behalf. Now both Moses and Aaron were of the tribe of Levi, and as

Figure 91 - Moses' rod becomes a serpent before pharaoh and his magicians

Aaron became the first High Priest, it was the Levites who were set apart for the priesthood from that time on.

Moses therefore returns to Egypt, but has difficulty persuading the Israelites that he is their savior, and with the help of Aaron and by performing the signs God gave him, they convince the Israelites to believe them. Moses and Aaron then go before the pharaoh and ask for the release of the Israelites in the famous phrase: "Let my people go." Pharaoh refuses, and thus begins the twelve famous plagues of Egypt, ending with the death of the first-born, including the pharaoh's son. The Israelite firstborn are spared because they follow the injunction to kill a year-old kid or lamb, eat it roasted with bitter herbs, and smear its blood on the doorposts and lintel; consequently, the Passover is instituted, as an annual memorial of the Jews' release from Egyptian captivity, and as the first sign of God's active involvement in the daily lives of the Children of Israel.

Figure 92 - Moses with the Ten Commandments. In reality there are 613 in the Bible!

Pharaoh relents and lets the Israelites leave, but then pursues them. Moses parts the Red Sea, and the Children of Israel are saved.

Early in their wanderings in the desert they arrive at Mount Sinai, and Moses ascends to commune with God. It is interesting that most people know that God gave Moses the Ten Commandments on the mountain, but little more. In fact Moses spent forty days upon the Mountain, and during this time God passed on a large number of laws to be followed, including most detailed instructions for the construction of the Ark of the Covenant, what it should contain, the holy vessels and the precise blueprints and assembly instructions for the tabernacle.

It is well worth reading Exodus, since within that relatively short book are detailed explanations of most of the characters and artifacts which features so prominently in the first part of this Degree.

It is also worth noting that, from the long lists of tribes and peoples the emigrant Israelites meet, trade with and fight during their travels, this region of the Near East was well populated by a large number of diverse cultures at that time.

At the end of his life Moses is permitted to see, but forbidden to enter the Holy Land. This may seem harsh indeed from a God who regularly proves so forgiving and indulgent towards the ungrateful Children of Israel, when Moses, who begged God to be allowed to enter that land, is denied his request. After all, he had faithfully followed every one of God's commands for well over forty years. However, one must remember that Moses stood in a special relationship with God: he is described as a prophet. On one occasion Moses allowed his temper to get the better of him, and in Numbers 20, we learn that, although God had told Moses precisely how to obtain water for the thirsty Israelites, Moses chose to add his own words and to strike the rock twice, an action God had not asked him to do. While this might seem a relatively minor infraction, for a prophet it was not: it was essential that a Prophet repeat the words God requires him to speak, without interpretation, adding or taking away from the message. Indeed, in Deuteronomy 18:20, God says: "But the prophet, which shall presume to speak a word in my name, which I have not commanded him

Figure 93 - The death of Moses

to speak, or that shall prophesy in the name of other gods, even that prophet shall die." So this was why Moses wasn't allowed to lead his people into the Promised Land.

Instead, it was his nominated successor, Joshua, who took the Children of Israel across the River Jordan.

Removing the Shoes

We saw that, when Moses encounters the burning bush, he is told by God: "put off thy shoes from off thy feet, for the place whereon thou standest is holy ground." (Exodus 3:5).

This action is to be seen in a number of religions. For example, you remove your shoes to enter a Mosque. You also remove them to enter a Hindu Temple. In part, the symbolism is one of removing the eternal clothing which attracts the most dirt and dust from the profane or outside world. This action is also reflected in the custom of bathing one's head, hands and feet prior to entering a holy site.

Figure 94 - Shoes outside a mosque

The story is repeated and acted out at the beginning of the Degree, for the Candidates wear sandals, which are removed at this point.

Seven Circuits

At the start of the ritual the Candidates make seven circuits of the Chapter. The first is made prior to the Obligation, upon their entrance as they are received under the living arch and make their way to the Western Altar. The second takes them to the diorama of the burning bush, at which point they remove their sandals.

Following the revelation of the burning bush their sandals are now replaced – at least in the modern version of the ritual.

The following three circuits continue the story of Moses up to the arrival of Joshua and the Children if Israel bearing the Ark of the Covenant into the Promised Land, and ends with the comment that, while they obeyed God's laws the people flourished.

At the sixth circuit they are told that, because the Israelites turned from God, they suffered the destruction of the Temple and city of Jerusalem, and were led away into captivity. But after seventy years they were freed by a Proclamation of Cyrus, King of Persia. The seventh and final circuit represents the exiles deciding to return to Jerusalem to assist in rebuilding the Temple, remembering the prophecy of Jeremiah 29:10 – 13.

However, in earlier versions of the ritual the circuits – or circumambulations – were rather more dramatic! Once the sandals had been removed at the burning bush, they remained off. Following the circuit describing the Jews being led into captivity, the Candidates were led out of the Chapter to simulate being led to Babylon. However, this was also a device to allow a unique piece of furniture to be set up. Called the 'rocky road', it consists of a number of pieces of flat wood, on which had been attached wooden bosses of varying sizes placed randomly upon them. This gave the 'road' a very uneven and treacherous surface to walk across – especially when blindfolded!

Figure 95 - The Cyrus cylinder, proclaiming the restoration of cult sanctuaries and repatriation of displaced peoples

The Proclamation of Cyrus was then read and the Candidates led into the Chapter, being advised that there were two routes to Jerusalem, and telling them to take the one through the wilderness to avoid being captured in the cities or towns. After prayer, they were warned that they were approaching a dangerous part of the road, and helped across the 'rugged road'. They performed this circuit three times, after which they were led out of the room as the Chapter continued with the Ceremony of Passing the Veils. The wording accompanying this very physical journey beautifully describe the passage from Babylon to Jerusalem:

"We are now on the green banks of the ever-running waters of the Euphrates. We are now passing through Syria, towards Damascus. We shall pass near the ancient city of Tamor or Palmyra, and through many beautiful groves and pleasant vineyards."

The journey ends with:

"But rough and ruggèd as was the road and long and toilsome as was the journey, it at last came to an end, and the weary sojourners were blest by the sight of the ruined walls of Jerusalem and the glistening tents of their Brethren. Here they turned aside to rest: here let us turn aside to rest and refresh ourselves."

In esoteric terms, this is often described as a *Pathworking*, which is sometimes defined as a technique of active imagination. Deprived of sight, the Candidates undergo a journey with physical stimuli (rocky road, circumambulations) while having scenes described to them which they can perceive in their mind's eye. This makes the experience very powerful since the Candidates are being allowed to relive the experience instead of simply being told about it. This technique is used throughout Masonic ritual, and a few minutes' contemplation on the Degree rituals will bring many examples to mind.

Although this dramatic journey is now but a memory in our modern ritual, it can still be seen performed each December in Ancient Chapter No. 1, which precedes the formation of the Grand Chapter of New York.

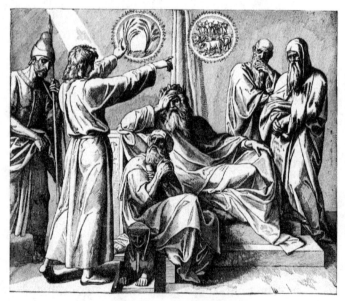

Figure 96 - Joseph interprets the pharaoh's dreams

Finally, the number seven itself is a powerful figure in both the Bible and in Freemasonry. This is the seventh Degree in the York Rite. There are seven days in a week; there were seven days in the story of Creation; and seven ancient planets. Indeed, the number seven was closely associated with divine perfection and the completion of a cycle. For example, we have Joseph's interpretation of the Pharaoh's dream of seven years of plenty followed by seven years of famine in Genesis 41: 1 – 32. To us the most important symbol is that of King Solomon's Temple being built in seven years. We mentioned in the section on the Most Excellent Master Degree that the circumambulations in that Degree reflected the six days in the story of creation, and now we have reached the seventh cycle, that of rest. As we saw, if is for this reason that the Temple is seen by many commentators to be a symbol of creation. And this is why it is also seen as a symbol for Man, with the three parts of the Temple relating to the three traditional parts of man, or the head (seat of the spirit), breast (seat of the heart) and trunk (seat of procreation). Or again the Holy of Holies, Holy Place and Courtyard have been assigned to spirit, soul and body.

The final, or seventh, circumambulation brings us to the entrance of the Tabernacle. As we approach the Master of the First Veil, armed with the password we learned from the image of the burning bush, we are again reminded how closely entwined are the stories of the Tabernacle in the Desert and the Tabernacle of Zerubbabel, which we are about enter.

To conclude this section, it is worth mentioning a theory put forward by Rev. Neville Barker Cryer, an English Masonic scholar. He suggests that the reason a story involving a return from exile would have been a popular theme at the time the rituals were crystallizing was because this was a major preoccupation in England at the time. Firstly, there was a wave of Jewish immigrants in the mid to late 17th Century seeking refuge during the Lord Protector's (Oliver Cromwell) time. Secondly this era saw the influx of Huguenots fleeing from France to Britain, and of course the Jacobites and Non-Jurors (those who refused to swear an Oath of Allegiance to William and Mary who came from Orange in what is now the Netherlands, to replace James II) fleeing in the opposite direction following the removal of King James II. This accords with the brief look at English History earlier in this section.

The Veils

The Veils are a representation of the Tabernacle. This part of the ceremony is a conflation of the stories of the Tabernacle, which was created under the instruction of Moses to contain the Ark of the Covenant, and the Second Temple, built on the ruins of King Solomon's Temple by his descendant Zerubbabel.

While there is no explicit mention in the admittedly sketchy descriptions of the rebuilding of the Second Temple in the Bible, the idea of the council meeting in a Tabernacle is quite plausible. It would have taken some years to rebuild the Temple and City, and the sacred vessels carried back from Babylon would have to have been stored somewhere inside. Since the leaders of the exiles included prophets, priests, scribes, and a prince, it is most likely they would have sought a solution from the Torah, Scribe Ezra (Esdras in Greek) is credited with bringing the Torah, or first five books of the Bible generally ascribed to Moses, back to Jerusalem following the exile, and would

Figure 97 - Interpretation of the Biblical description of the veil showing all four colors and cherubim motif

have had an extensive knowledge of them. It would be likely they would seek a solution to their problem in the sacred writings, and were inspired to create a second Tabernacle following the precise instructions in Exodus, in which it was explained how to create and store the Holy vessels.

While Exodus 26:31 seems to suggest there is but a single veil between the outer court and the Holy Place, the colors listed to be included are: blue, purple, red, and 'fine twisted linen'. While this fourth color is normally interpreted as being white, during the recent refurbishment of the Chapter Room at New York Grand Lodge, this curtain was replaced by a linen-style curtain which, being off-white, more accurately reflects the original description.

If we examine the layout of the tabernacle as a whole, we find three veils, two of which later become walls in King Solomon's Temple. The first admits us into the outer courtyard; the second into the area reserved for priests; and the third into the Holy of Holies. However, these do not have unique colors according to the Bible.

In the Royal Arch Ritual, the four veils are used as barriers to entry, and the Candidate must first negotiate his way through the four veils before finally arriving in the presence of the Grand Council. Symbolically they have been referred to the levels of progress in Masonry, to the four elements, and to the trials of Moses.

Figure 98 - Ham, Shem and Japheth with Noah from the Nuremburg Chronicles

In this case the veils, which match the colors of the four banners, are used to draw attention to the close association between the Blue and Red Lodges, as we pass from the color blue, indicating Operative Masonry, purple, indicating an admixture of blue and red to show the 'intimate connection' between Blue and Capitular Masonry, and finally to red, showing that the Candidate has now passed into the realm of the Royal Arch, also evidenced by the fact that the password are the names of those associated with the rebuilding of the Temple. Finally, the fourth veil is white, and is also used as a device to show us we are now moving beyond the three Degrees and onto a fourth level.

The First Veil, guarded by the Master of the First Veil, is negotiated by giving the Password of the Degree, which he heard given during the diorama of Moses and the Burning Bush. Here he is given the passwords and actions to pass the succeeding veils. In some traditions the reference to Ham, Seth and Japheth recalls Noah's Ark as the 'Ark of Safety'.

The Second Veil sees Moses, Aholiab and Bezaleel referenced and their creation of the 'Ark of Testimony'. And let us not forget that Moses was found in an Ark hidden in the bulrushes by an Egyptian princess.

The Master of the Third Veil mentions the Grand Council who presided over the Ark of the Covenant rediscovered.

At the Fourth Veil, in addition to the passwords and sign, he is also asked to present the Ring to show that he is indeed worthy to approach the Grand Council.

The perceptive student may notice a couple of anomalies here.

Firstly, if the white veil gives access to 'the Sanctuary of our Sacred Tabernacle', surely that should separate the Holy of Holies, which only the High Priest was allowed to enter. Firstly, the Ark of the Covenant had not be discovered at this point in the ritual, so no disrespect was being committed. Secondly, while they were following the layout of the Tabernacle, there was no reason they couldn't adapt the

Figure 99 - Bezaleel and Aholiab work on the Tabernacle and its furnishings

design to their own present needs, and since they had no expectation that the Ark would be found and the True Name discovered at that time, having an inner court where the ruler could sit, well protected from the enemies who the Bible tells us continually harassed the Jews while they tried to rebuild their city and Temple.

Indeed, while the modern day English ritual no longer uses the veils, the Bristol Rite does. In this case the veil ceremony is performed in a room outside the Chapter room, and the white veil hung over its door, so that, having gone through the ritual of Passing the Veils, and having received the password needed to enter the Chapter, the Candidate finally passes through the white veil into the Chapter Room, which here represents the Sanctuary for this portion of the rite.

The second question might arise over why the Sojourner would present Zerubbabel's ring if Zerubbabel himself were seated within the Sanctuary! While the symbolism of the signet ring is discussed later, suffice it to note at this point that a monarch or ruler would have a number of

Figure 100 - Jeshua, Zerubbabel and Haggai

signets produced to give to his delegates working in different parts of the kingdom and as ambassadors to other countries. Here we may imagine that Zerubbabel had given a number of rings to different tribes or groups who would travel separately back to Jerusalem, and this would be a clear sign that they were to be trusted before being let into the presence of the Grand Council.

In our ritual, however, the ring is held by the Master of the Third Veil which he then presents to the Candidate to give to the Royal Arch Captain guarding the Fourth Veil. While this seems illogical, it was probably a stage direction changed at some time to avoid the Principal Sojourner or a Candidate having to carry it from the beginning of the ceremony.

Although the veils are blue, purple, red and white, like the banners to which they allude they also refer to the four principal tribes (as we shall see in the sections on the banners below):

- The First Veil is blue and the banner represents the tribe of Dan, symbolized by the Eagle.
- The Second Veil is purple and the banner represents the tribe of Reuben, symbolized by Man.
- The Third Veil is red and the banner represents the tribe of Ephraim, symbolized by the Ox.[3]
- The Fourth Veil is white, and the banner represents the tribe of Judah, symbolized by the Lion.

There is a final attribution of the veils which we might consider. The first great Covenant of God with His people was that with Noah and his progeny, upon the blue waters, with his Arch of seven colors (reflecting the seven lights of the menorah or the seven planets) in the heavens. This reminds us of the Blue Veil. The second great Covenant was between God and Abraham, whom God tells "I will make of thee a great nation, and I will bless thee and make thy name great" (Genesis 12: 1 – 2). The covenant is sealed by Melchizedek the High Priest, who gives him bread and wine. This Royal Covenant is symbolized by the Purple Veil. The third great Covenant was that with the

---

[3] Note that this is the lineup in the vast majority of States and Countries. For reasons which are unclear, Ephraim and Reuben are reversed in New York. Given that this is a the logical order, this has been retained here even if it differs in New York

Children of Israel and Moses, and was the Covenant borne of the blood with which they painted the lintels of their houses to indicate their trust in Yahweh. This is symbolized by the Red Veil. The last great covenant may be drawn from Revelations, perhaps, in which we read: "And I saw a new heaven and a new earth: for the first heaven and the first earth were passed away; and there was no more sea. And I John saw the holy city, New Jerusalem, coming down from God out of heaven, prepared as a bride adorned for her husband." (Revelation 21: 1 - 2). Note that we have progressed from flood, sea, river to 'no more sea'. At each Covenant, the waters become less. Now there is no separation between us and God. And the Veil which must be drawn for us to enter into the presence of the great I AM is bridal white. We will come across this 'diminution' again a little later.

It should be stressed that these colors are unique to United States Royal Arch, and do not accord with the Bible what the Talmudists say, or even the Canadian Royal Arch! However, using the American version for now, the Eagle (sometimes symbolized by the Scorpion or Snake) has long been associated with the classical element of Water; Man with Air; the Ox with Earth; and the Lion with Fire. Much has been written on these symbols; but since the attribution of color to each Tribe is very variable, any symbolic association should be undertaken with caution!

The Signs

The Signs come from Exodus 4: 1 – 9, and are given between the First and Second, Second and Third, and Third and Fourth Veils. Each refers to the three Signs Moses was told to give to the Children of Israel in order to convince them that it was truly God who had send him to them to lead them out of captivity. Again, the number three is used to great effect in the Bible. In this case the people deny Moses three times, which is often used by those who seek to link the Old and New Testaments to reflect Peter denying he knew Jesus three times before the cock crowed. It is as if, as well as the password, the Candidate must convince each Master of the Veil that he is indeed coming as a representative of God by repeating the miraculous signs Moses gave to the Israelites in order to gain access to the next Veil. The three signs are of a rod turning into a serpent (and back again), a hand turning white and leprous (and back again), and water turning into blood. In a way this reflects the grip and word of the Blue Lodge Degrees, in that a word is not sufficient: a physical sign must also be given in order to be admitted to the next level.

Once again, we see the melding together of the story of Moses and the Story of Zerubbabel. It is only at the fourth veil that the Mosaic references are finally set completely aside and we move several hundred years forward in the action.

The Banners

JUDAH   EPHRAIM   REUBEN   DAN

Fig. 103 – The Four Banners

We are taught that the four banners represent the principle tribes of Israel. Yet they are really representative of all Twelve Tribes of Israel, which marched in a set order during the sojourn in the desert under Moses and Aaron, and which camped in a set pattern about the Tabernacles as it traveled whenever the caravanserai halted. Indeed, in other Royal Arch traditions, notably in England and Scotland, all twelve banners are present.

These tribes have long been equated with the twelve months and twelve signs of the zodiac in the Zohar, a second century C.E. book attributed to Rabbi Shimon bar Yochai, yet reflecting teachings which went back much earlier. Astrology also features extensively in Talmudic teaching.

When the twelve tribes of Israel marched out of Egypt under Moses, and through the desert, they were divided into four groups, each under a leading tribe. The four main tribes were Judah (accompanied by Issachar and Zebulon), next Reuben (accompanied by Simeon and Gad), then Ephraim (accompanied by Manasseh and Benjamin), and finally Dan (accompanied by Asher and Naphthali). When they camped, the ordered themselves with Judah in the East, Reuben in the South, Ephraim in the West and Dan in the North.

Very early on the commentators linked the twelve tribes with the months, and the groups of three tribes with the four seasons. This also meant that they linked them to the signs of the zodiac, a device begun with the ancient Mesopotamians, who had divided the night sky into twelve bands of 30° in order to mark the seasons, and therefore the times to plant the crops – an important advance in knowledge for a people which had changed from a migratory to a sedentary society. At a very early stage the four main tribes were associated with particular signs: Judah with what we now know as Leo or the Lion, Reuben with Aquarius or Man, Ephraim with Taurus or the Ox, and Dan with Scorpio or the Eagle (a common interchange in early times of astrology). The early

Jewish scholars also associated the nine minor tribes with the other Zodiacal signs, thought their associations have been debated by scholars for centuries. However, the associations of the four principal tribes probably comes from Genesis Chapters 48 and 49. In these Israel (or Jacob) blesses his sons (actually he tells them what horrible futures they will have!), effectively setting the layout of Israel under the tribes.

Ephraim is recognized as the first tribe, telling him to 'increase greatly on the earth." One could suggest that this gave Ephraim the kingdom of earth, which is often represented by the sign of the Ox. However, in Deuteronomy 33:17, where Jacob blesses his sons, he says "His glory is like the firstling of his bullock, and his horns are like the horns of unicorns: with them he shall push the people together to the ends of the earth: and they are the ten thousands of Ephraim." This is certainly a clearer association of Ephraim with the Ox.

Reuben is identified in Jacob's blessings as his firstborn – a man (Genesis 49:2). Judah is identified as a "lion's whelp" (Genesis 49:9); and finally, Dan is called "a serpent", which was often associated with the scorpion, and as explained above, therefore with the eagle (Genesis 49:16).

Another point worthy of mention is, while Judah was seen as the 'protecting' tribe, the *primus inter pares* was still the first to receive Jacob's blessing in Genesis 48 – Ephraim. Remember that, due to the procession of the equinoxes, that wobble of the earth's axis which means different Zodiacal signs rise at the spring equinox to begin the year every few thousand years, at that time it was Taurus which led the zodiacal procession across the heavens, a point which some have mystically associated with the fact that this was a time of intense animal sacrifice – especially bulls. Those same scholars have pointed out the contemporaneous timing of the Minoan culture, which also sacrificed bulls.

Figure 104 - Tympanum on a church in Arles, France

Later, this symbolism was extended into the New Testament, with the four Evangelists represented in art by the same four animals: Matthew as the man, Mark as the lion, Luke as the ox, and John as the eagle.

The idea that the four principal tribes represented Man, Lion, Ox and Eagle is important because Hebrew scholars through the millennia have sought to draw parallels through the biblical texts. In this case we now see that, during the Exodus, around the Tabernacle, which was seen as the seat of God, were stationed the Lion, the Man, the Ox and the Eagle, in the four quarters. This of course refers to Ezekiel 1:10 and 10:14, and Revelations 4:7. So the banners of the "four principal tribes of Israel we use in Chapter have a very profound message, which goes beyond the fat that these tribes led the Israelites out of bondage and protected the tabernacles when the encampment was at rest: they represent the very avatars which surrounded the throne of God, of which the Tabernacle was an earthly representation.

And finally, we should not forget that, when George Washington, the first President of the United States, took the Presidential Oath, he chose this very passage – Genesis Chapters 48 and 49 – on which to lay his hand when taking his oath. Some have suggested the Bible was opened at random. It seems unlikely, given that the entire ceremony was planned by Masons well-versed in the Volume of the Sacred Law! Perhaps he chose the passage because it talked of the founding of a new Nation, which brought twelve sons and a father together – and there were thirteen colonies uniting to create a Nation State. But then he

Figure 105 - George Washington Inaugural Bible opened at Genesis, Verse 49

was also a Mason, and initiated in the Lodge in Fredericksburg, the very Lodge whose records reflect the first Royal Arch Degree being worked in the New World.

Shem, Ham and Japheth

Shem, Ham and Japheth were the sons of Noah, who, with their wives, went into the Ark with him and thus became the only survivors of the Flood.

Figure 106 - Engraving of Noah's Ark from the Nuremburg Chronicle

It may seem odd that they would be mentioned in the Royal Arch Degree. It must be remembered that the Holy Royal Arch Degree took its sources from a number of earlier rituals. One of these was – and is – called the Royal Ark Mariner Degree, and is based on the story of the Ark, and features these character in the ceremony. It is also believed by many scholars that this Degree originated in the Mystery or Miracle Plays performed by the guilds outside cathedrals and churches on Holy Days for the entertainment and education of the masses. It should be remembered that in earlier times the only language used in church was Latin, and the majority of the public being illiterate, the Miracle Plays were their main source of learning the more famous Biblical stories.

A key feature of this Degree was the rainbow, being God's promise and *covenant* with His people stretching across the sky.

Indeed, another consideration is how all these stories are about journeys to find some form of Truth. In the story of Noah, the ark (incidentally, in many language the word for 'ark' and 'arch' is the same), a group of people are carried over the waters by an Ark to Ararat, a safe haven. In the story of Moses and the Chosen People, an Ark (of the Covenant) is carried across the earth by men, on their way to the Land of Milk and Honey. In the story of the Rebuilding of the Temple, the descendants of Israel travel a dangerous and rocky road, carrying the vessels of the destroyed First Temple

Figure 107 - Noah offers a sacrifice to God (one hopes he had three of whatever he sacrificed on board...)

from the East (Babylon) to the West (Jerusalem) with the intention of rebuilding the House of God.

As an aside, it is also curious to note that in each case we see a reiteration which, like ripples on a pond, become less with each repetition. In the story of Noah, his family are on a flood which covers the earth; in Exodus Moses parts a sea; and in the return to Jerusalem the remnants of Israel cross a river (the Jordan). Or again, if the Temple is an image of Creation, then we move from God's abode in Eden, with a garden adjacent in which lived Adam and Eve; then God lives in a vast Temple; and finally, in a rather smaller Temple erected on the ruins of the greater by a band of emigrants. Once again, we have this theme of 'diminution' as man and God communicate on an increasingly even level.

It is therefore not difficult to see how this symbol of the Arch, together with the key players, made its way into early forms of the Royal Arch Degree.

Moses, Aholiab and Bezaleel

To better understand why these three characters feature in the Royal Arch Degree, it is useful to recall the short Catechism said at all Royal Arch Festive Boards in England:

- "Companion Principal Sojourner, how many Grand Lodges do we commemorate?
- "Three, Most Excellent.
- "Name them.
- "The First or Holy Lodge, the Second or Sacred Lodge, and the Third or Grand and Royal Lodge.
- "Where was the First or Holy Lodge held?
- "At the foot of Mount Horeb, in the wilderness of Sinai.
- "Who presided?
- "Moses, Aholiab and Bezaleel.
- "Where was the Second or Sacred Lodge held?
- "In the bosom of the Holy Mount Moriah.
- "Who presided?
- "Solomon, King of Israel, Hiram, King of Tyre, and Hiram Tyrian, Widow's Son.
- "Where was the Third or Grand and Royal Lodge held?
- "At Jerusalem.
- "Who presided?
- "Zerubbabel, prince of the people; Haggai, the prophet; and Jeshua, the son of Josedech, the high priest."

It is interesting to note that our ritual covers both the travels of Moses and those of Zerubbabel, while the story of King Solomon is absent, having been covered in the Master Mason Degree. A possible reason for this has been reviewed in the section *Possible Connection to the Third Degree* above.

Moses, of course, was the prophet who led the Israelites out of captivity into the desert, who organized the tribes during that journey, and who supervised the creation and erection of the Tabernacle, assigning the Tribes to the duties ascribed to it. It was he who dictated the design of the Tabernacle and the creation of the holy vessels, the primary ones being the Altar of Incense, the Seven-branched Candlestick, the Table of Shewbread and, of course, the Ark of the Covenant. It was also he who placed an omer of manna, Aaron's rod, and a copy of the Law received from God into the Ark.

In Exodus 31 we learn God called Bezaleel from the tribe of Judah and Aholiab of the tribe of Dan (two of the four principal tribes) to serve him. The description of their skills is remarkably similar to those of Hiram Abif, filling them: "in wisdom, in understanding, in knowledge, and in all manner of workmanship, to design artistic works, to work in gold, in silver, in bronze, in cutting jewels for setting, in carving wood…" (Exodus 31, 7 – 11).

Figure 101 - The Seven-Branched Candelabra of the Temple as spoils of war on Trajan's Column in Rome

Bezaleel and Aholiab are to make: "The tabernacle of meeting, the ark of the Testimony and the mercy seat that is on it, and all the furniture of the tabernacle; the table and its utensils, the pure gold lampstand with all its utensils, the altar of incense, the altar of burnt offering with all its utensils, and the laver and its base; the garments of ministry, the holy garments for Aaron the priest and the garments of his sons, to minister as priests, and the anointing oil and sweet incense for the holy place." (Exodus 31, 12 – 17).

Since Bezaleel and Aholiab are therefore going to work closely with Moses in creating the Tabernacle and all the furniture within, and since the two of them will provide and craft the objects under the supervision of Moses, it becomes apparent why their relationship is similar to that of King Solomon, who supervised, with Hiram King of Tyre, who provided, and Hiram Abif, who crafted. Remember, too, that Bezaleel and Aholiab were senior members of two of the four principal tribes, and therefore carried respect and authority in their own right. Since early Freemasonry came to see this triumvirate as the rulers of the "First or Holy Lodge", it is not surprising therefore that we still encounter them in the Royal Arch Degree, since they were the creators of the objects associated with the Ark which are brought to light in this Degree.

Jeshua, Zerubbabel and Haggai

We are familiar with these characters, since it is Jeshua who governs the Chapter as High Priest, Zerubabbel who assists him as King, and Haggai who competed the Grand Council as Scribe. In fact, in the Old Testament, Haggai is Prophet to Zerubbabel, and it is he who rouses Zerubbabel to speak with King Darius to seek permission to return to Jerusalem, as we read in the Book of Haggai. However, the Bible is unclear whether he actually returns with Zerubbabel and Jeshua, both of whom lead the remnants of the Israelites back to Jerusalem. We read of Zerubbabel in the Books of Ezra, Nehemiah and 1 Chronicles; and in the Prophecies of Haggai and Zechariah. The clearest description of the journey and rebuilding of the Temple are to be found in Ezra, here returning under the authority of King Cyrus of Persia, rather than Darius.

We also find brief mentions in two Apocryphal books, Sirach and I Esdras. It is in Esdras that we find the famous debate over the power of wine, women, and the king, in which Zerubbabel declares that Truth is greater than all things, and in terms of our ritual this joins his name to the concept of truth, so that the ring or signet with which he is presented by Cyrus as evidence of his royal commission is called the "ring of Zerubbabel, or Truth."

Figure 102 - Zerubbabel receives authority from King Cyrus to return to Jerusalem

As we saw above, this is the Third, or Grand and Royal Lodge presided over by Jeshua, Zerubbabel and Haggai.

In fact, it is worth perhaps noting that, since we are descended from Operative Masons, in all three cases the rulers meet in Lodges, not Palaces, Temples or Throne Rooms.

The Signet

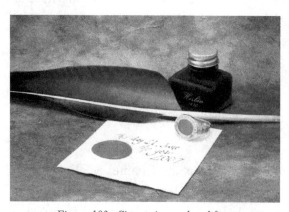

Figure 103 - Signet ring and seal from www.foxfirejewelers.com

The use of a signet ring, which bore a seal, was a common method of sealing treaties and official documents from early in man's history. A document would be prepared, then melted wax poured upon it and the ring impressed in the wax to form a seal, which would attest to the document's authenticity. This was both an enduring symbol of authority, and also a useful measure when the monarch was often illiterate and incapable of writing his own name.

As a symbol of authority, the ruler's signet was often reproduced, either perfectly or with qualifying signs, and circulated to those who had authority over regions of his land, so that satraps, princes or minor rulers could issue local edicts in the name of the king. This led to the practice of giving a ring bearing the monarch's seal to those who needed to travel across his lands, as a sign to those guarding the cities or places of passage that he traveled with official permission. While official papers were often issued for this purpose, a ring indicated the travelers had the personal permission of the ruler, and therefore should be allowed to pass without hindrance.

Note that the pharaoh gave a signet ring to Joseph when he put him in charge of protecting Egypt from the predicted famine (Genesis 41: 41 – 42).

In the Royal Arch the signet represents the fact that the traveler has the permission of Zerubbabel. This is of course unlikely, since there is no reason a prince would give his ring to a latecomer to the Exodus from Babylon to Jerusalem, nor even a copy of it. However, in the Degree the ring has a second purpose: to remind us that Zerubbabel stands for Truth, and that by implication those who bear his ring are both seeking an audience with the Sanhedrin for a high purpose, and that their endeavors will bring about the discovery of Truth, or the True Word. In this it is a commonly used plot device, where a small object is a harbinger of future action.

Where does this idea come from? In Hebrew, the word 'truth' is *emet* or *emeth* (אמת). Jewish sages noted that these three letters, *aleph*, *mem* and *tav* (remember Hebrew is written right to left) are also the last letters of the three words which conclude the account of Creation, '*bara Elohim la'asot*' (ברא אלהים לעשות). These three letters (*aleph*, *mem* and *tav*) also mark the beginning, middle and end of the Hebrew alphabet. According to the Jewish sages, "the seal of God is Truth", a phrase which should be very familiar to us by now. In this context, *emet* is seen as the experience of self-fulfillment, of completing God's plan for mankind. In one Kabbalistic commentary, it is described as being "the power to realize one's own deepest potential, which is in fact the power of the Jewish soul to bring about the ultimate realization of God's potential."

It is interesting to see just how profound the background to this symbol in the Royal Arch truly is. It is yet another proof that these rituals were not lightly thrown together, but were assembled by men who were deeply versed in all manner of religious, spiritual, esoteric and historical subjects, who were determined to preserve this ancient wisdom in our rituals. We are fortunate indeed to have this treasury of philosophical and practical teachings to study.

Candlestick, Altar of Incense, Breastplate and Ark of the Covenant

If you read Exodus Chapter 25, you will find a detailed description of the Tabernacle, the Ark of the Covenant, the Breastplate, and the Seven-Branched Candlestick, the Table of Shewbread (which oddly is not mentioned at all in our ritual). Chapters 26 and 27 read almost like a modern craftwork manual in its detailed description of the building of the Tabernacle, adding that these plans were given to Moses along with the Ten Commandments on top of Mount Sinai.

The Breastplate – or *Breastplate of Judgment* to give its full title – which is still worn by the Presiding Officer in most Chapters is described as a plate of gold into which are set four rows of three stones, each engraved with the name of one of the twelve tribes of Israel.

The Seven-branched Candlestick – or Menorah – was made according to a design provided by God to Moses. It is perhaps interesting to note that all the elements of the candlestick were to be made of beaten gold. As well as being a precious metal, it is also an inert metal and a very good conductor. One may perhaps wonder how such an imposing item could be made out of solid gold, since the Israelites were meant to have fled during the night from Egypt, and it would be hard to imagine their first thought was

Figure 104 - High Priest's Breastplate

to how much gold they could carry, especially since they were slaves and therefore unlikely to possess much. This is awkwardly handled in the Bible in Exodus 3:22, where it says God told Moses to get the Israelites to 'borrow' as much silver, gold and cloth as they can manage to obtain from their Egyptian neighbors, which is later put towards the building of the Tabernacle. This 'borrowing' is rather like that college roommate we all dreaded, who seemed to think our belongings were also his to use or wear!

One may also remember that, during Moses' absence communing with God, they persuaded Aaron to make a golden calf out of their jewelry, which was later melted down into ash and the Israelites made to drink it in water (Exodus 32:1 – 20). It is also noteworthy that the seven arms are to be decorated with almond blossoms and almond buds – reminiscent of Aaron's wand which was later placed in the Ark. By the time the Menorah was placed in the Temple, it had nine companions, since we are told in II Chronicles 4:7 that King Solomon (who did nothing by halves) had no less than ten Seven-branched Candlesticks placed in the Temple.

The Menorah was filled with the purest olive oil, and was never allowed to go out. This practice is continued in many religious traditions, including Christian churches and synagogue, as a symbol of the eternal presence of God within the sanctuary. It is also seen as a memorial to the dead, where the eternal flame is often present at Tombs to the Unknown Solider seen in many countries (incidentally the first eternal flame ever to commemorate an individual as opposed to an unknown warrior was that placed upon the tomb of President John F. Kennedy).

Figure 105 - Table of Shewbread

For the sake of completeness, although it is not mentioned in our ritual, the Table of Shewbread bore twelve loaves of bread, made of flour according to a recipe known to the Priests, and placed in two columns of six, surmounted by cups of frankincense. The Table was placed to the North of the Altar of Incense, while the Menorah was placed to its South. The bread was replaced weekly, and wine was poured over them, in a ceremony which reminds us of the offering of the first High Priest mentioned in the Bible, Melchizedek, to Abram (Genesis 14:18), which will be well-known to those who have received the Order of High Priesthood, a prerequisite to being allowed to officiate as the High Priest of a Chapter, and which in New York State is performed once a year during the Annual Convocation of Grand Chapter.

The Altar of Incense is described in Exodus Chapter 30. It was a double cubical altar set immediately before the veil in front of the Holy of Holies, and incense was continually burned upon it. Like the Ark it was made of Shittim Wood, which is a species of Acacia, and as every Mason knows a symbol of immortality. Both were covered with a layer of gold, and both the Ark and Altar had rings set into them and two gold-covered staves, presumably to carry them in processions, not unlike the God Thrones of ancient Egypt, on which they were probably modeled, since the Israelites had lived in captivity in Egypt for many years and would have logically drawn much of their religious symbolism from that country's practices and customs.

Figure 106 - Altar of Incense: note the rings and staves similar to the Ark of the Covenant

The Ark of the Covenant we saw for the first time in the Most Excellent Master Degree, when it was 'safely seated' in the Holy of Holies during that ceremony.

Figure 107 - Realization of the Ark of the Covenant at the Washington Masonic Memorial, Alexandria, VA

The presence of the Ark of the Covenant in the Royal Arch ritual is largely Masonic license, since there is no reference to it in the Bible after the sack and destruction of Jerusalem by Nebuchadnezzar. It is also not featured upon Trajan's column in Rome, which commemorates the sack of the Temple in C.E. 66, in which only the Menorah is pictured. There is a telling story in the Talmud, the authoritative body of Jewish tradition, of a priest finding a loose stone on the Temple Mount and, realizing it is where the Ark was hidden, runs to tell his colleagues, but dies on the way. The moral is, that the Ark is not yet meant to be found. This common tradition of something remaining lost until it is meant to found can also be seen in the legend of King Arthur, and, of course, the Lost Word.

However, despite the debate over whether it featured in the Second Temple built by Zerubbabel, its importance as a Masonic symbol is profound, since it is the vehicle by which the True Word is recovered: it bears the Word upon its exterior, while within is found a cipher through which is learned how to pronounce that Word.

The form of the Ark is also different to that used in the Most Excellent Master Degree. While the one used in that ceremony is closer to the precise descriptions in Exodus, including the Mercy Seat and the two Cherubim, the one used in the Holy Royal Arch Degree omits the Mercy Seat and Cherubim; perhaps to make the story of finding the characters upon it and removing the lid to discover its contents simpler to follow.

While the High Priest traditionally wears the breastplate at all meetings of the Chapter, this version of the Ark of the Covenant, Menorah and Altar of Incense are normally only used during the Royal Arch Degree Ceremony itself.

In the ritual, it is assumed that the Menorah and Altar of Incense were brought back to Jerusalem from Babylon by the exiles as part of the furnishings of the Temple handed over by King Darius; while the Ark of the Covenant was found beneath the ruins of the Temple during the ceremony, to accomplish the words of the Master Mason Degree: "until the wisdom of future generations discovers and brings to light the True Word."

The Prophecy

As the Candidates come before the High Council, the High Priest reads from Haggai 2:1 – 9, 23.

This is a bridge passage, which recalls how Zerubbabel the Prince and Jeshua the High Priest were inspired to lead the remnants of the exiled Israelites back to Jerusalem to rebuild the city and Temple. It recalls God's Covenant with his people when He led them out of exile in Egypt, and now reflected in the journey out of exile in Babylon. It is interesting to note that, in the passage, we are told that God said: "The glory of this latter house shall be greater than of the former." However, we also read in Ezra 3:12 – 13 that: "many of the priests and Levites and chief of the fathers, who were ancient men, that had seen the first house, when the foundation of this house was laid before their eyes, wept with a loud voice; and many shouted aloud for joy: So that the people could not discern the noise of the shout of joy from the noise of the weeping of the people: for the people shouted with a loud shout, and the noise was heard afar off." In other words, those who were too young to remember the glory of the first temple shouted for joy, but those who remembered King Solomon's Temple wept when they saw the Second Temple being erected by Zerubbabel and Jeshua.

In our ritual, the Scribe is Haggai. In the Bible, however, he is called a Prophet; and in the English ritual the three members of the High Council are Zerubbabel the King, Jeshua the Priest and Haggai the Prophet. The English ritual also had two scribes – Ezra and Nehemiah, which reflects the fact that they both wrote about the second temple, notwithstanding the fact that they were by no means contemporaries!

The Task & the Sojourners

Figure 108 - Lowered into the vault

In many versions of the Holy Royal Arch Ritual the three Candidates are referred to as Sojourners. The term 'sojourner' means someone who is a traveler, but is staying temporarily in one place. Thus, the Candidates, who have traveled from Babylon to Jerusalem are now invited to rest awhile, and assist in the work being undertaken. They are told that the only work remaining is menial, and involves clearing away the rubbish in order to lay the new foundations for the Second Temple. Symbolically, this indicates that, although they have just proven themselves to be Most Excellent Masters, or the most sophisticated and accomplished Masons, they are told they must undertake the type of work normally given to Entered Apprentices. However, they willingly accept the task in hand, for they have been taught that "he that humbleth himself shall be exalted": and we know that in a little while these humble sojourners will indeed be Exalted (the Ceremony of the Holy Royal Arch is sometimes called 'Exaltation') to become the Masters of the Veils.

The task itself, clearing away rubbish in order to lay the new foundation, is of course symbolic. In several continental versions of this degree, including the Scottish Rectified Rite and the Rite of Strict Observance, the Latin motto associated with this degree is *'Adhuc stat'*, meaning "It still stands". This is accompanied by a Tracing Board depicting the fallen Temple, but with the pavement and the bases of the two columns still standing. Here we can see the fallen Temple as a version of Hiram Abif. The man was murdered, but the Inner Man, that part which makes him immortal could not be destroyed. Similarly, the physical Temple may lie in ruins, but that essential part, the immortal soul of the Temple, still exists, and this is why the ceremony has the Sojourners enter the very heart of the edifice in order to discover the great secret, that eternal part of the Temple which man alone cannot destroy.

Figure 109 - The foundations of the First Temple still stand

Again, if the Temple is a symbol for our own bodies, now dead and corrupt, what is this rubbish which we are clearing away? It is the accretion of bad behavior, dissipation, sinfulness, pride, envy, indeed all those attributes which we have been working to chip away in order to reveal the perfect ashlar within. Now we clear away these 'extraneous knobs and excrescences.' And what do we find? The Ark within! At last we understand: Truth lies within. It is not some distant external goal. It was been within us all the time, but we failed to recognize it.

The Working Tools

Figure 110 - Sojourners' tools

The tools the Sojourners are given are the crow(bar), pickaxe and the spade. We are told that the crowbar is used to lift objects of great weight – in this case the capstone of the vault. The pickaxe is used to loosen the soil and the spade is used to dig up and cast aside the rubbish.

We are also told that these refer to lifting prejudice and passion from our minds, loosening the hold of sin and folly, or vice and ignorance, and preparing the ground upon which to build the spiritual and moral life of his Second Temple.

In the English ritual, their description is rather more evocative:

"The stroke of the pick reminds us of the Last Trump, when the grave shall be shaken and loosened and give up its dead; the crow, being an emblem of uprightness, points out the erect manner in which we shall arise on that awful day to meet our tremendous though merciful Judge; while the manner in which the body is laid in the grave is depicted by the work of the shovel."

It is perhaps interesting to note that in the Popular National Songster, a collection of patriotic and other songs written in the early 1800s, one song, called *Patriotic Diggers*, which was meant to evoke a sense of class equality:

Figure 111 - Popular early 19th Century song

Johnny Bull beware, keep at a proper distance,
Else we'll make you stare at our firm resistance,
Let alone the lads who are freedom tasting,
Recollect our dads gave you once a basting.

Chorus:
Pick-axe, shovel, spade, crow-bar, hoe and barrow,
Better not invade, Yankees have the marrow.

To protect our rights, 'gainst your flints and triggers,
See on yonder heights our patriotic diggers,
Men of every age, colour, rank, profession,
Ardently engag'd, labour in succession.

Chorus:
Pick-axe, shovel, spade, crow-bar, etc...

...

Here the Mason builds freedom's shrine of glory,
While the Painter gilds the immortal story;
Blacksmiths catch the flame, Grocers feel the spirit,
Printers share the fame and record their merit.

Chorus:
Pick-axe, shovel, spade, crow-bar, etc...

It is difficult not to be struck by what appear to be clear references to Masonry hidden in this song. Firstly there is the overt claim that Masons were responsible for freedom and the war against *John Bull*, or the English. Though other trades are listed, their function is rather to extol and preserve the tale of the Masons' efforts. It is also interesting to note that the Chorus lists the pick-axe, spade (shovel is but a variation) and crowbar. It also says: "Yankees have the marrow". While this may be a stretch, it would seem to be a close hint at possession of a secret. In *The Origins of Freemasonry: Scotland's Century, 1590 – 1710*, by David Stevenson, he says (page 149): "The form *marrow bone* was also influential in the eighteenth century, and was incorporated with the Hiramic Legend: the secret taken from the corpse was a bone, with the marrow or secret in it."

Figure 112 - The sword and trowel

Traditionally there are two other tools which were used by the builders of the Second Temple. While not overtly mentioned in the Preston Webb Royal Arch Ritual, they are commonly found in almost all other variants of the Royal Arch theme, and are even mentioned in the Cryptic Degrees, which once say alongside the Capitular Degrees. These are the sword and trowel, and are taken from Nehemiah 4:14, which says: "The laborers who carried the loads worked with one hand and held a weapon with the other." So, the workmen carried a trowel with which they rebuilt the Temple, and a sword in the other hand, with which they defended themselves from their enemies who sought to prevent them from finishing.

Figure 113 - Remember that the two towers in front of cathedrals (here Notre Dame in Paris) reproduce Boaz and Jachin, or the pylons before the Egyptian Temples...

Symbolically the sword and the trowel also represent the Tree of Life, reflected in the two columns of King Solomon's Temple. The sword represents the Pillar of Severity, while the trowel indicates the Pillar of Mercy. Recall its introduction as a Working Tool of the Third Degree, when we are told it is used for: "spreading the cement of brotherly love and affection, that cement which unites us into one sacred band of friends and Brothers."

The Inventions or Discoveries

We learn, not surprisingly, that there are three discoveries. The first is the Keystone, the second the three Squares, and the third the Ark of the Covenant. Each discovery links it to one of the preceding Capitular Degrees.

Firstly, the Keystone is found, which was discovered among the rubbish in the Mark Degree, and is once more discovered among the rubbish in this Degree.

Secondly the three Squares are discovered, which reminds us of the Virtual Past Master Degree, since the Square jewel is the insignia of Mastership.

Finally, Ark of the Covenant is found; and as we learned in Hiram King of Tyre's speech in the Most Excellent Master Degree: "although the structure has been finished, the Temple is not complete, for it cannot be the House of God until the Ark of the Covenant has been placed therein."

For Masons, while the discovery of the Ark is of great importance, it is almost incidental in our story to the most important discovery of all: the True Word.

Figure 114 - Edward Kelley, John Dee's assistant, reanimating a corpse

The True Word is written within the very heart of the Temple. In the Mark Degree we hear Revelations 2:17 quoted: "To him that overcometh will I give to eat of the hidden manna, and will give him a white stone, and in the stone a new name written, which no man knoweth saving he that receiveth it."

We learn that, just as man has his true name written within, so does the Temple, and by finding and saying this word the Temple – like man – may be brought back to spiritual life.

The power of a name has been taught across the centuries. In magical lore, it was taught that, in order to control a person, angel or even demon one needed to know its true name. This is why, in the Rite of Exorcism, one of the priest's main tasks is to get the inimical spirit possessing the victim to divulge its true name. Once the priest has this he can go about the task of expelling it from the person it is occupying. Vodoun has a similar ritual for controlling another person through knowing his or her name. Even seemingly harmless Victorian love spells involved writing the name of the object of desire upon a piece of parchment and performing some innocent spells over it, then either wearing the paper in a locket or burying it in a place the desired one would walk over. Angels, demons, sprites, elementals, even gods have been summoned through the ages by evocation, which meant using their name. Even our fairy stories and nursery rhymes reflect this action: think of Rumpelstiltskin, or the Wicked Witch's mirror in Sleeping Beauty to cite just two examples.

It is hardly surprising, therefore, that in this story the name which will reestablish the Temple is found at the very heart of the ruins, and that uttering it will bring the whole edifice back to life.

The Substitute Ark and the Substitute Word

As an aside, it is worth noting that the Ritual is careful to state that the Ark of the Covenant is a *copy*, and the contents *imitations* of the pot of manna, Aaron's rod and the book of the Law. This problem is neatly sidestepped in other Royal Arch rituals. For example, in England, it is the word which is found on a double cubical altar, and not the Ark. Similarly, in some European rituals, the focus is upon rekindling the sacred fire to represent the return of God/life to the Temple/Man.

The passing mention that these are replicas themselves is completely incidental to the story, and is only included to provide continuity with the story of the Cryptic Degrees, which are a part of the York Rite family in the United States and some other countries. The point of the story is that of discovering a great secret within the vault of the old Temple, by means of which the True Word is recovered, and the 'wisdom of former generations' restored.

The symbols found within the Ark are taken directly from the description of the contents in the Holy Bible, and are reflected in the Capitular Degrees. The manna is referred to in the passage describing the white stone upon which a name is written. The rod reflects that carried by the Principal Sojourner as a staff of office, that of Moses which became a snake before the Children of Israel and before the pharaoh's Priests; and that of Aaron when it budded to indicate that he had been selected as the High Priest. Finally, the Book of the Law reflects the belief that Ezra reintroduced the Pentateuch, or Torah in Jerusalem, upon the return of the exiles. This contained the books ascribed to Moses, being Genesis, Deuteronomy, Exodus, Leviticus and Numbers. We can also note that the Book of the Law represents the Scribe, the Pot of Manna the King (he who feeds and provides for his people), and Aaron's Rod the High Priest.

Finally, by means of the Ark and the key found within, the Substitute Word is abrogated, and the True Word rediscovered and conferred upon the Candidates. Henceforth they are Companions, in possession of that which was lost.

And they are finally taught the reason why Hiram Abif couldn't communicate the Master's Word to the ruffians. It was not stubbornness which prevented him. Of course there was bravery, but more than anything it was the physical impossibility of transmitting the word as it requires three people in the proper position in order to communicate the True Word. Once he was dead, King Solomon and Hiram King of Tyre could no longer utter the word themselves since, according to Masonic tradition, it could only be uttered by the High Priest in the Holy of Holies but once a year, or by three Master Masons each uttering but a single syllable of that word.

The Masonic Alphabet

The Masonic code or Pigpen code, as it is also known, despite the admonition in the ritual to destroy it after explaining how the words on the Ark are derived, can hardly be said to be secret any longer. It is found in Dan Brown's 2009 novel *The Lost Symbol*, and even in children's books as an easy substitution code. A simple search on the internet will reveal not only the code laid out for all to see, but even fonts which you can download and use on your computer!

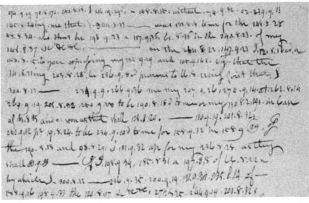

Figure 115 - Part of Benedict Arnold's coded letter to John André

However, there is evidence that this cipher played a much more serious role in the late 17th and early 18th Century. There is evidence that George Washington's army used the system, but with the letter of the alphabet more randomly associated with the signs, and it was also used during the Civil War by union prisoners in Confederate jails. We may see it on many Masonic gravestones of that period, too. And there is evidence it was used in communications between Masons which they wished to keep private.

The Discovery of the True Mason's Word

The actual word itself works particularly well in the context of the ritual. As we just learned, since the Word could only be uttered completely by the High Priest once a year in the Tabernacle, and later in the Temple, the only other people who could utter it were King Solomon, Hiram King of Tyre, and Hiram Abif with a 'tribble voice'. When Hiram Abif was slain the ability to pronounce

129

the Word was lost, and it was lost a second time – this time to the Children of Israel – when Judah was overrun by Nebuzaradan, Captain of the Guard to Nebuchadnezzar.

While Masonic lore is unclear on the matter, it is assumed that, since the High Priest could only teach his successor the Great and Sacred Name of God, this avenue of restoring the Lost Word was forever closed to King Solomon and Hiram, King of Tyre.

Figure 116 - The Kingdoms of Israel and Judah

We should remember that Israel only remained united as a people for a very short time. When King Solomon's son, Rehoboam, came to the throne, the people of Israel begged him to lighten the taxes which King Solomon had put on them to pay for the Temple and his palace. But Rehoboam received bad advice from his young friends, and ignoring the counsel of the elders, uttered the famous line: "My father made your yoke heavy, but I will add thereto: my father chastised you with whips, but I will chastise you with scorpions." (2 Chronicles 10:14). So the majority of the people separated themselves, and two countries were established: Judah in the Southern part, which included Jerusalem, and was composed of the tribes of Judah and Benjamin; and Israel, to the North, which was composed of the other ten tribes.

In Masonic lore the Word was lost to us when Hiram Abif was killed; and in the Bible it was lost to the people of Judah when the Temple was razed to the ground.

It is interesting to note that, while the means of discovery – called the Grand Royal Arch Word – is recited at every meeting of Royal Arch Masons, becoming in itself a kind of second substitute word, the Great and Sacred Name of God is only uttered when the Holy Royal Arch Degree is being conferred upon Candidates. Since most Chapters will probably only confer the Degree once a year, this holds true to the idea that the Great and Sacred Name should only be uttered but once a year in the Holy of Holies.

Exaltation

It is interesting to see that the word *exaltation* has two meaning in England. Firstly, it is "the act of raising someone or something in importance." Secondly, it is "a strong sense of happiness, power, or importance." (both Merriam-Webster dictionary). www.dictionary.com goes on to include "elation of mind or feeling; mystical exaltation."

Both would seem to be highly appropriate, in that they reflect both an external and internal transformation.

Externally the Candidate is now called a Companion rather than a Brother. He is no longer a Sojourner, but a permanent resident of Jerusalem, with an important and prestigious role in guarding the High Council seated in the Tabernacle. He is now symbolically a Master of a Veil. Since three must be Exalted at one time, this means the three new Companions now become the Masters of the Blue, Purple and Red Veils, under the instruction of the Royal Arch Captain. The new Companion is now in possession of the True Word of Master Mason. His old white apron has been removed and a more glorious one, trimmed with red and bearing a potent sigil upon its flap, tied about his waist.

Figure 117 - In England and in its Jurisdictions the apron is more elaborate, and a sash is also worn

Internally, he is overjoyed with the discovery of the True Word, and his elation is matched by the knowledge that he has symbolically completed his Masonic journey, that he is now perfected, his Living Stone now forms part of the fabric of the Spiritual Temple, and within him he carries that Name which no man may know, save him to whom it is given. He has died and passed beyond the veil. He has seen God face to face, and knows His Name.

But in all this euphoria, we must remember an important fact. Initiation, by its very definition, means a beginning, it does not make one an Adept; it only provides permission or authority to study to become that person which he has symbolically represented in the ritual itself. The Companion has been given the tools, but if he lays them aside, believing that he is now a perfect man, he fools himself and submits himself to the tyrannical sin of pride or *hubris*. His new journey is now only beginning. He has passed through the veil and now his learning, his path begins anew. It is now for him to gird himself with his sword, take his trowel in hand, and continue on this magnificent journey of discovery.

The Words

The words used to learn the pronunciation of the Great and Sacred Name, we are told, are "composed of the names of Deity in three languages, the Syriac, the Chaldean and the Egyptian."

Why are these three languages – or countries – selected?

Figure 118 - Chaldean inscription c. 500 BCE

Conveniently for Masonry, and its love of the number three, the Children of Israel are associated with three major journeys. The first was the journey out of Egyptian bondage and into the Promised Land. The second was the journey which led from Jerusalem into exile in Babylon under Nebuchadnezzar, of the Chaldean dynasty. Finally, the Children of Israel returned to Jerusalem empowered by the initial ruling of King Darius I, King of Persia, who adopted the Aramaic language of Syriac as the official language for all legal and political communication and documents across his empire.

It is interesting to note that all three of these tongues were associated with quasi-monotheistic religions. However, early Masonic scholarship was not what it is now, and so we find as few minor errors in what is otherwise a clever device: the rediscovery of how to pronounce the True Name of God by aid of the names of the 'head' Gods of the three countries in which the Children of Israel formerly sojourned.

We are told that 'Jah' is the name of the Syriac god. In fact, this is unlikely, since Darius and Cyrus were almost certainly Zoroastrians. Apart from a healthy respect for the Judaic god, who among other names, was called 'Jah', the uncreated father-god of the Zoroastrians was Ahuramazda.

We are on firmer ground with the Chaldean *Bel*. This is another name for Marduk, who was the god of the Babylonian region and considered the leader of the gods.

Figure 119 - Marduk, or Bel

Unfortunately, with the Egyptian God we are back on shaky ground. We must remember that the translation of the Rosetta Stone – which provided a passage in hieroglyphs, demotic Egyptian and Greek, enabling hieroglyphic inscriptions to be translated – did not take place until 1822, and the first English translation was not until 1854. Prior to that time ancient Egyptian history was largely guesswork and fantasy.

In Genesis 41:45 we read that, in recognition of interpreting the pharaoh's dream, Joseph is given Asenath, the daughter of Potiphar (sometimes rendered Potipherah), priest of *On*. It is highly likely that this is where the idea that On was a great god in Egypt arose. Initially – and incorrectly – On was thought to be an old name for Osiris. However, later scholarship revealed that On was in fact a place, not the name of a god! The true father of the Egyptian gods was Ra.

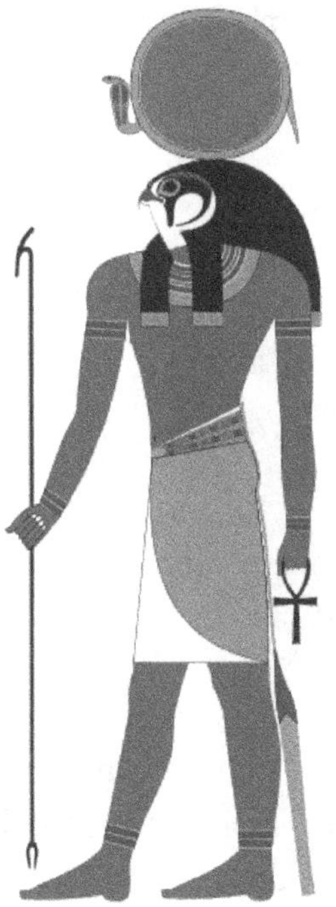

One thing in common between the gods is that they are all solar gods – associated with the sun. This recalls the position the sojourner's hand involuntarily took in order to protect his eyes when recovering the Ark.

Figure 120 – Ra or Re, the Sun god of the Egyptians

The Number Three

We have seen a number of instances of the number three in this Degree, which continues the litany of threes in the Blue Lodge Degrees. Indeed, the list at the end of the Historical Lecture may be read with profit.

However, there is a particular application of the number three which is prominent in this Degree, yet not explicitly mentioned in that list. At the Opening of the Chapter, the High Priest asks the Captain of the Host: "How shall I know you to be a Royal Arch Mason". The response is: "By three times three."

Now, we know there are three times three, or three groups of three Officers – the High Council, the three subordinate Officers (Captain of the Host, Principal Sojourner, Royal Arch Captain) and three Masters of the Veils. There are three times three passwords to pass through the Veils, and we put our right feet, left and right arms in a three times three position in order to communicate the Word.

However, there is a subtler force at work. Three times three can also be expressed as three squared, or 3^2. If the regular symbolism of the Blue Lodge is the repetition of the number three, we now see this squared to nine. We can say mathematically that the number three is now functioning at a higher power. This is another indication that this Degree is suggestive of a higher level, or plane: as we have seen before, in the Royal Arch we have moved from the terrestrial, earthly plane to the spiritual plane.

The Triple Tau

Figure 121 - The Royal Arch Emblem

Surely there can be no more fascinating and mysterious symbol than the emblem of this Grade: the Triple Tau, contained within a triangle within a circle. We are told that this device is "the emblem of emblems of a Royal Arch Mason, typifying the Sacred Name, the Author of Eternal Life."

This is a somewhat terse description of so profound a symbol.

In the English Ritual we are taught in the Mystical Lecture that: "The triangle has long been considered a sacred symbol. In times of antiquity names of God and symbols of the Deity were often enclosed in triangular figures. The Circle, having neither beginning nor ending, is an emblem of eternity, and may justly be deemed a symbol of God, without beginning of days or ending of years…"

However, on the subject of the Triple Tau it is less helpful:

"The Tau is that mark or character spoken of by the angel whom Ezekiel saw in the spirit, when it was said to the man with the writer's inkhorn: 'go through the midst of the city, through the midst of Jerusalem, and set a mark upon the foreheads of the men that sigh and that cry for all the abominations that be done in the midst thereof'; by which mark they were saved from among those who were slain for their idolatry by the wrathful displeasure of the Most High.

"The Tau was in ancient times set upon those who were acquitted by their judges, as a proof of their innocence, and military commanders caused it to be placed on those who returned from battle unhurt from the field of battle, to show that they were in perfect life. It has, therefore, even been considered a mark or sign of life. The union of the three Taus alludes to the Deity, by whom the gloom, horrific, and unshapen chaos was changed into regular form and peaceful existence."

Very poetic, but it still doesn't tell us why we would wear this mark upon our apron!

Figure 122 - Nehustan, the Brazen Serpent

The tau is both the 19th letter of the Greek alphabet, and also the 22nd letter of the Hebrew alphabet. In this context, the Hebrew *tau* or *tav* is more pertinent. The 22nd Path of the Tree of Life links Malkuth, or Earth, to Yesod, or the Astral, and to attain that level you must pass through a veil. Another name for Yesod is Foundation, and this is what is being restored and rebuilt in the story of the Royal Arch Degree. It is also considered to represent a cross – not the Christian one with four arms, but the T-shaped cross Moses erected in the desert bearing the Brazen Serpent Nehushtan (Numbers 21:9).

Being the last letter in the Hebrew alphabet it also signifies ending, or a new beginning. Three Taus represent this emphatically. It is the symbol of the absolute, of the perfection of creation; and since it bears the highest value of any Hebrew letter, 400, it also stands for infinity.

In the form of the Greek *tau*, which may have been the original shape of the Hebrew tau, or the cross carried by Moses, in the passage from Ezekiel (9:4) mentioned above, it is a sign of absolution from sin, which is a similar purpose to the snake upon the cross of Moses, since many commentaries identify the snakes which plague the Children with Israel with sin, and gazing upon the brazen serpent on the cross as an act of contrition, and therefore absolution., symbolized by the comment that those who gazed upon it did not die. Naturally, in Christian commentaries, that later led to this scene in the desert being seen as a harbinger of Jesus hanging upon the cross, bearing the weight of mankind's sins, and that those who gazed upon the cross – that is, turned to Christianity – would have everlasting life. However, we should also remember that the introduction of the cross as a symbol of Christianity was relatively late, not coming into common imagery until the 4th Century C.E. Prior to that it was more common to use the symbol of a fish, or the Chi-Rho symbol, since the cross was an awkward reminder of the ignominious death, reserved to slaves and traitors, which the Nazarene had suffered.

Esoterically the letter *tau* represents a gateway or opening (since its later appearance looked like two doorposts with a lintel across them), or a symbolic death leading to a new life; an initiation including a symbolic death, such as was practiced in many of the ancient mystery cults – and Freemasonry! In this sense, the link between gateway and cross become obvious, since *tav* is the last letter of the alphabet, signifying the end, but a new beginning. A doorway symbolizes moving into a new place. And the cross symbolizes death to a new life, be it the painful torture or gazing upon a brazen serpent as a promise to live like a new man.

Figure 123 - Celestial Jerusalem descending from heaven

Some see the emblem of the Triple Tau as actually being a letter 'T' standing upon a letter 'H'. This is been severally identified with the phrase 'Templum Hierosolyma", Latin for the Temple of Jerusalem; and even the initials of Thoth, the great Egyptian teacher, who was meant to have brought the knowledge of the gods to mankind; and who was also believed to be Hermes Trismegistus, the legendary sage. In the Mark Master Degree, we learned that the device written upon the Keystone began with the letters 'HT' indicating Hiram (the) Tyrian.

Perhaps the most important lesson to learn is that the Masonic sign par excellence, the point within a circle, is now expanded in form and meaning. We are taught here that the Brother is the point and the circle Deity, and also the boundary of his duty to God and man. In this system man was at the center. Now in the Triple Tau God is at the center, and we contemplate Him, not as an external power, as we did in the earlier Degrees, but now as a part of us, within us, ruling and guiding our actions.

This God within, bears three essential attributes, as we are told in the Historical Lecture, like the triangle, to represent the three essential attributes of God, namely Omnipresence, Omniscience, and Omnipotence.

The Symbol of the Holy Royal Arch

The Arch itself is a very profound symbol indeed. It has many interpretations, but perhaps the clearest one may be considered here.

We understand that the arch completes the edifice, and also the roof to be placed over the building to cover the inner space. It was in understanding the nature of arches that the Egyptians, then the

Israelites and all nations of the Middle East, the Greeks, the Romans, and the Masons of the Gothic era and later were able to build ever taller structures with larger and larger protected interiors. So the columns raise the walls, the arch holds the ceiling in place, but the keystone binds the whole together.

The inspiration for this architectural structure, as we have seen, probably came from a close observation of the Book of Nature, and columns closely resemble the tree trunks which are still used in more primitive tribes as the verticals which form the framework of the walls, while the idea of the vaulted ceiling probably came from an observation of the way the higher branches became interwoven in forest canopies.

For us, we recognize the columns of Boaz and Jachin as representing the terrestrial and celestial worlds. Indeed, in our Lodge Rooms 'B' bears a terrestrial globe, while 'J' bears a representation of the heavens or celestial realm.

Figure 124 - The terrestrial and celestial pillars

What was once one in God became divided into two. This theme of division may be seen everywhere: male and female, day and night, good and bad, rich and poor, summer and winter. Everywhere in Nature we see two contending forces. Our entire Masonic journey has been spent trying to find how to reconcile these two forces.

Perhaps the most perfect and simple image of two contrary forces being reconciled is the triangle, or delta. It teaches us that a third side, or force, is required to balance the other two and make them harmonious and whole. This is perhaps why the delta has for so long been both a symbol of deity, and an indication of a reconciliation of three forces which comprise God. Most theologies contain some form of Trinity, from Isis, Osiris and Horus; and Shiva, Vishnu, and Brahma; right down to Father, Son and Holy Spirit.

Another is the arch.

If Boaz represents the Earth and Jachin the Heavens, then what does the Ark which unites them represent? It is the Ark of the Covenant, the arch of the rainbow, that which united God and Man. Since we have become separated through man's pride and his fall, then we can work to rebuild the path, the Jacob's Ladder which used to unite us. In the Arch, we reconcile heaven and earth, and open the path of communication between them once more.

The Keystone which holds the bond between heaven and earth conjoined and co-dependent is the very stone with the builders rejected. With it we bridge the gap, and all of us become a pontifex, or bridge-builder. This is the fifth or final Alliance which will be everlasting.

Figure 125 - The Roman Catholic Pontifex - then and now

And one last thought to ponder. Upon the surface of that White Stone which holds the bridge between heaven and earth in place, is a name composed of eight letters, as we learned in the Mark Master Degree.

H∴T∴W∴S∴S∴T∴K∴S

The number eight is considered the number of perfection in many esoteric systems. For example, in Nicomachus' Arthmetic, it is equated with universal harmony. It is also the third number of the celestial triad in the Qabalistic Tree of life (Kether being '10' and Binah '9'), and therefore represents the Eternal Son, or again Perfected Man who finally aspires to join with God. And Man is perfected through Truth, or *emet*…

And finally, we learn why this degree is called the Holy Royal Arch, when the Arch appears to feature so little in the story. For this is a story of recovering the Lost Word, of discovering Truth within ourselves once more. And armed with self-knowledge and knowing the True Name of the Great and Ever-Living God, we may dare to cross the bridge which separates us from Him.

The Charge

The Charge reminds us of our duties as Royal Arch Masons and Companions. It gives us three admonitions.

Firstly, that we are to study those lessons we have just received, and which should have profoundly impressed us. We should have realized that we are entering a completely different level of understanding of the lessons of Masonry, and have begun to realize there are indeed important secrets in Freemasonry which remain hidden to those who are not prepared to take the time to study and understand them.

Secondly, we are given an indication of the way we can accomplish this difficult goal. We are told to 'contemplate' the Sacred Source, and to 'realize more and more the ever presence of the Great I Am'. This is a progressive study, borne of contemplation or meditation. It is not enough to sit and read: one must allow the teachings to infiltrate us, to move us, to become one with us, until we intuitively begin to understand the messages within the Degree which have only been touched on in in this course.

And thirdly, we are told to guard the Outer Door more carefully than ever. We are not to cast pearls before swine. These Mysteries – and the Charge openly uses the word 'Mysteries' are only to be unveiled to those who have the capacity to learn from them. The outer courts of the Blue Lodge have their foundations in the earthly world. The Royal Arch establishes its foundations in the spiritual world. We have symbolically died, with Hiram, in order to pass to this Second Temple, and, like him, we have endured that Long Night of the Soul and merited coming before the Throne. And now we must keep the Veils between the two systems firmly drawn, and only part them when we find a person who is worthy to join this honorable Order of Companions.

Biblical References

As in the previous Degrees, the system of Capitular Degrees draws very heavily from both the Old and the New Testament. Although the stories told in the ritual are from the Old Testament, many lessons are drawn from the Gospels. This should not be very surprising. Firstly, these rituals came from countries which were heavily steeped in the Christian tradition. Secondly, these Degrees concern themselves with the fulfilment of promises made by God, and the perfection of Man who may now rise above his sinful nature and reunite with God. These are surely themes found in abundance in the New Testament.

Yet in the 18th Degree of the Ancient Accepted Scottish Rite, when we are told that the story of Jesus is used to teach the Law of Love, we are also reminded that people of all religions should not fail to see the message in this story and apply it to their own paths. Similarly, this is a story of man perfecting himself.

In this it uses the references to Jesus in an almost gnostic sense: that we all contain a spark of the divine, and that however immersed in mud and slime we become, in taking on an earthly body, as Adam did when he turned from God, that spark lives on, immortal and undiminished. If we take the trouble to recognize our potential, and work upon ourselves, making us fit receptacles of that immortal fire, or spiritual temples not made with hands, as our ritual says, then we may once more shed our earthly body and find ourselves clothed in that Glorious Body which was our First Estate, and commune once more with the God from whom we came, the Great Architect of the Universe Who made us, and who by that act of creation became forever our Father in Heaven.

You will find that throughout this course all biblical quotations or citations have been followed by the relevant chapter or verse in the Volume of Sacred Law. For ease of reference the name of the book has always been written in full, followed by the number of the chapter, and verse. For example, Ezekiel 2:22 – 24 would mean the Book of Ezekiel, Chapter 2 Verses 22 to 24.

If you are familiar with the Bible and are a regular reader, we hope this course have given you food for thought. If you are less familiar with the Holy Book, we would remind you of the Worshipful Master's admonition right after your Obligation as Entered Apprentice: "Freemasonry, therefore, opens this book upon its Altars, with the command to each of its votaries that he diligently study therein to learn the way to everlasting life."

Now you understand why these words are both so important, and how they were, even then, a harbinger of the journey which would lead to this Degree. You have symbolically died and been raised, set aside all substitutes and been entrusted with the Truth, the True Word. You have the tools, and we have explained them as much as we are permitted. The rest of the journey is up to you!

HRA Quiz #4

1   How many Officers are required to open a Chapter?
(a) 3.
(b) 7.
(c) 9.
(d) 10.

2   What are the colors of the four veils?
(a) Red, White, Blue and Black.
(b) Red, White, Blue and Purple.
(c) Red, Green, Yellow and Black.
(d) Blue, Purple, White and Green.

3   How do Candidates first enter the Chapter?
(a) On the step of a Most Excellent Master.
(b) Carrying a Keystone.
(c) One foot slipshod.
(d) Under a Living Arch.

4   Which Officers don't wear swords?
(a) The Veils.
(b) The Captain of the Host and the Principal Sojourner.
(c) The High Council and the Principal Sojourner.
(d) All of them wear swords.

5   Where is the Obligation taken?
(a) On an altar in the West.
(b) On an altar in the East.
(c) On an altar in the center of the Chapter.
(d) On an altar in the Northeast.

6   Where are the Candidates symbolically traveling from?
(a) From Egypt to the Promised Land.
(b) From Jerusalem to Babylon.
(c) From Babylon to Jerusalem.
(d) From Joppa to Jerusalem.

7   What to the four veils represent?
(a) The Palace of the Egyptian pharaoh.
(b) The Tabernacle.
(c) The Temple of King Solomon.
(d) The Holy of Holies.

8   What do you associate with the words of the Master of the First Veil?
(a) Noah's Ark.
(b) The Tabernacle.
(c) The Pillar of Fire and Cloud.
(d) The Rebuilders of the Temple.

9   Who issued the Proclamation freeing the Children of Israel?
(a) Nebuchadnezzar.
(b) Jeshua.
(c) Darius.
(d) Cyrus.

10   Who led the Children of Israel into the Promised Land?
(a) Moses.
(b) Joshua.
(c) Aaron.
(d) David.

11   What happened when Moses cast his rod upon the ground?
(a) It turned into a serpent.
(b) It sprouted buds, blossomed and yielded almonds.
(c) It broke.
(d) It turned into water.

12   What does the Menorah or Seven-branched Candlestick alight in the Southeast of the Sanctuary represent?
(a) The rainbow.
(b) The seven planets.
(c) The seven days of the week.
(d) All of the above.

13   Whom do the High Council represent?

(a) Moses, Aaron and Bezaleel.

(b) Jeshua, Zerubbabel and Haggai.

(c) Solomon King of Israel, Hiram King of Tyre and Hiram Abif.

(d) The Maccabees.

14   What are the Working Tools of a Royal Arch Mason?

(a) Gavel, chisel and plumbline.

(b) Axe, shovel and rope.

(c) Crow(bar), pickaxe and spade.

(d) None of the above.

15   What was the second discovery the Sojourners made?

(a) The Keystone.

(b) The Ark of the Covenant.

(c) A dead squirrel.

(d) Three squares.

16   What does *Anno Depositionis*, or the Year of Deposit mean?

(a) The year King Solomon's Temple was completed.

(b) The year the cornerstone of King Solomon's Temple was laid.

(c) The year Zerubbabel started to rebuild the Temple.

(d) The year the Children of Israel returned to Jerusalem from Babylon.

17   What here languages composed the names of God on the sides of the triangle on top of the Ark?

(a) Greek, Aramaic and Hebrew.

(b) Aramaic, Syriac and Egyptian.

(c) Chaldean, Egyptian, Syriac.

(d) Hebrew, Syriac and Chaldean.

18   Which tribes were taken into captivity in Babylon?

(a) Judah, Reuben, Ephraim and Dan.

(b) Levi.

(c) All twelve tribes.

(d) Judah and Benjamin.

19 What are the essential attributes of Deity?
(a) Faith, Hope and Charity.
(b) Omnipresence, Omniscience and Omnipotence.
(c) Justice, Temperance, Fortitude and Prudence.
(d) The lion, man, the eagle and the ox.

20 What mathematical symbol has often been used to symbolize deity?
(a) The triangle.
(b) The circle.
(c) The point.
(d) All the above.

21 Why was it impossible for Hiram to give the ruffians the Master's Word?
(a) His throat had been cut across.
(b) He was not the High Priest.
(c) His integrity prevented him.
(d) It could only be written down.

22 What animal symbolized the tribe of Dan?
(a) The lion.
(b) Man.
(c) The ox.
(d) The eagle.

23 To what does Grand Hailing Sign of Distress allude?
(a) Dessication.
(b) Drowning.
(c) Evisceration.
(d) Amputation.

24 How any circumambulations are there in this Degree?
(a) 4.
(b) 6.
(c) 7.
(d) 9.

25   On what Book and Chapter did George Washington take his Oath as first President of the United States?

(a) Genesis Chapter 1: 'In the beginning God Created the Heaven and Earth.'

(b) Genesis Chapter 49: 'Jacob calls and blesses his sons.'

(c) 2 Chronicles Chapter 2: 'King Solomon determines to build a Temple to God.'

(d) John Chapter 1: 'In the beginning was the Word.'

26   What were the three Grand Lodges called?

(a) The First Lodge, the Second Lodge, and the Third Lodge.

(b) The Grand Lodge, the Royal Lodge, and the Lodge of Exile.

(c) Moses' Lodge, Solomon's Lodge and Zerubbabel's Lodge

(d) The Holy Lodge, the Sacred Lodge, and the Royal Lodge.

27   What implements tell us that the Israelites were harassed as they tried to rebuild the Temple?

(a) The sword and trowel.

(b) The gavel and trowel.

(c) The sword and buckler.

(d) The rod and sword.

28   What is the Pentateuch?

(a) The first five rulers of Israel.

(b) The first five books of the Bible, attributed to Moses.

(c) The ancient Elements.

(d) The stones in the High Priest's breastplate.

29   What is the name of the ritual which creates a Companion?

(a) Raising.

(b) Elevation.

(c) Consecration.

(d) Exaltation.

30   Which body is sovereign over the Chapters in a State?

(a) Grand Chapter.

(b) General Grand Chapter.

(c) Grand Council.

(d) Grand Guignol.

31   In which year was the Grand Chapter of New York established?
      (a) 1789.
      (b) 1798.
      (c) 1803.
      (d) 1813.

32   Where are the oldest Minutes of a Royal Arch meeting recorded?
      (a) In Fredericksburg Lodge, Bristol, UK.
      (b) In Stirling Chapter, Scotland, UK.
      (c) In Fredericksburg Lodge, Virginia, US.
      (d) St. Andrew's Royal Arch Chapter, Massachusetts, US.

33   "How shall I know you to be a Royal Arch Mason?"
      (a) By the perfect points of my entrance.
      (b) By the Living Arch.
      (c) By three times three.
      (d) By grip and word.

HRA Discussion Questions

1   We have seen that the number '7' has a strong connection with the Holy Royal Arch Degree. List the number of instances of the number '7' being used in the Degree, in the ritual, in its symbols and by implication. Why is the number '7' so important in the Royal Arch, and what does it teach us?

2   Consider the Seven Liberal Arts and Sciences covered in the Middle Chamber Lecture. They are: Grammar, Rhetoric, Logic, Arithmetic, Geometry, Astronomy and Music. How are these used in the Royal Arch Degree? Can you detect their presence and their influence? Identify parts of the ritual which exemplify each Art and Science.

3   The four veils have been seen as symbols for a great number of concepts, ranging from the four elements to the four faces of the Merkabah of Ezekiel and Revelations. Review those allegories and interpretations mentioned in this course, and critique them. What do you think of them? Can you think of any others?

4   We learned that there were a number of possible antecedents to the Royal Arch Degree, including the story of Noah's Ark, which still features in the Royal Ark Mariner Degrees of the Allied Masonic Degrees; and the pseudepigraphical Book of Enoch, which contained both references to nine subterranean vaults concealing a white porphyry stone bearing the ineffable name of Deity, and the two columns of marble and brick bearing the wisdom of humanity to withstand conflagration or inundation. Think of another story in the Bible which would lend itself to a Masonic Degree. How would you stage it, and what lesson would it transmit?

5   Do you think there is any credibility in the theory that the Royal Arch Degree was originally part of the Installation Ceremony, and that its symbolism was removed for political reasons? What do *you* think the origins of the Royal Arch Degree were?

Figure 126 - English Royal Arch Tracing Board. The Ritual is slightly different but most of the symbols displayed are common to the York Rite

Recommended Reading

Primary focus on American Freemasonry:

The History and Symbolism of Royal Arch Masonry, by Edward E. Graham, pub. 2000 by 1st Books Library, ISBN 0-75964-091-2

A History of Royal Arch Masonry Part One, by Everett R. Turnbull and Ray V. Denslow, pub.1955, reprinted 2010 by Kessinger, ISBN 1-4179-5004-8.

A History of Royal Arch Masonry Part Two, by Everett R. Turnbull and Ray V. Denslow, pub.1955, reprinted 2010 by Kessinger, ISBN 1-4179-5005-6

A History of Royal Arch Masonry Part Three, by Everett R. Turnbull and Ray V. Denslow, pub.1955, reprinted 2010 by Kessinger, ISBN 1-4179-5006-4

Guide To The Royal Arch Chapter, by John Sheville and James L. Gould, pub. 1867, reprinted 1981 by Macoy, ISBN 0-88053-021-9

Proceedings of the Grand Chapter of Royal Arch Masons of the State of New York, Vol 1. 1798 – 1853, pub. 1871 by Grand Chapter State of New York, (no ISBN)

Proceedings of the Grand Chapter of Royal Arch Masons of the State of New York, Vol. 2.1854 – 1867, pub. 1871 by Grand Chapter State of New York, (no ISBN)

The Book of the Chapter, by Albert Mackey, pub. 1863. Available online (free) at: books.google.com/books?id=JH9JAAAAIAAJ

The Freemason's Monitor or Illustrations of Masonry, by Thomas Smith Webb, pub. 1979, republished in 1802 with sections on Capitular Masonry, the Order of High Priesthood and Orders of Knighthood. Available online (free) at: www.coloradofreemasons.org/pdfDocuments/library/TheFreemasonsMonitor.pdf

Royal Arch Companion Adapted to the Work and Lectures of Royal Arch Masonry, by Alfred F. Chapman, pub. 1904, reprinted 2010 by Kessinger, ISBN 0-7661-0072-3

Thomas Smith Webb – Freemason, Musician, Entrepreneur, by Herbert T. Leyland, pub. 1965 by Otterbein Press, (no ISBN)

More general books on Capitular Masonry, Europe, History, etc.:

Freemasons Book of the Royal Arch, by Bernard E. Jones, pub 1957. Available online (free) at: www.phoenixmasonry.org/freemasons_book_of_the_royal_arch.htm

Tell Me More About the Mark Degree, by Rev. Neville Barker Cryer, pub. 2007 by Lewis Masonic, ISBN 978-0-85318-278-8

The Mark Degree, by Bernard H. Springett, pub. 1968 by London: A. Lewis, (no ISBN)

The Pocket History of Freemasonry, by Fred L. Pick and G. Norman Knight, revised and updated by Frederick Smyth, pub. 1977 by Frederick Muller Ltd., ISBN 0-584-10256-9

The Royal Arch Journey, by Rev. Neville Barker Cryer, pub. 2009 by Lewis Masonic, ISBN 978-0-85318-331-0

What Do You Know About the Royal Arch?, by Rev. Neville Barker Cryer, pub. 2002 by Lewis Masonic, ISBN 978-0-85318-227-6

Other courses:

The Chancellor Robert R. Livingston Library: reading course 12 on Capitular Masonry: www.nymasoniclibrary.org/library/courses.htm

Companion Adept of the Temple course offered by the York Rite Sovereign College of North America: www.yrscna.org/forms/YorkRiteenrollmentform.pdf

Resources specific to New York State (but available to all Royal Arch Masons):

NYRAM – a regular Magazine for New York Companions and friend, providing news, dates and events. Sing up to receive it on the Grand Chapter Website.

Grand Chapter Website at www.ny-royal-arch.org, a go-to place for all things Royal Arch, from calendar dates, contact details, downloadable documents and even the shopping boutique!

APPENDIX – ALLEGORY OF VIRTUAL PAST MASTER DEGREE

The Allegory was composed by E∴ Howard, L. M. Jones, PHP of Unity Chapter No. 16, Dayton, Ohio in 1942, and approved for optional adoption in the Virtual Past Master Degree by General Grand Chapter.

The Allegory takes place immediately after the Grip and Word of Past Master have been exchanged by the RWM and SD. The RWM returns to his station in the East, and the Candidate is conducted by the SD to a seat among his Brethren in the North, after which the SD returns to his place.

RWM Brother Junior Warden, call the Craft from labor to refreshment.

JW *** Brethren, it is the order of the Right Worshipful Master that you be called from labor to refreshment, until the sound of the gavel in the East.

*The lights are now turned down to represent the hour of midnight in the Temple. The Right Worshipful Master leaves his Station and is seated on the sidelines. Two guards are placed at each of the three Gates – East, West and South – dressed in uniforms in keeping with their work. When these Officers, or guards, are in their places, the lights are turned up half way. The Right Worshipful Master, Senior and Junior Wardens act as the three Grand Masters: Solomon, King of Israel, Hiram, King of Tyre, and Levi (**not** Hiram Abif) as the third. Levi is a workman from the quarries. All but the last character are dressed to represent men in their later years (old age) – that is, Solomon and Hiram of Tyre are so represented; Levi is a much younger man.*

King Solomon proposes to discuss certain matters of importance with Hiram. This is done in low tones so that no-one hears the conversation (done in pantomime). While they are thus engaged in conversation, Levi, a Craftsman, enters and endeavors to work his way to the Secret Chamber to speak to the two kings. After passing the three Gates and the guards stationed there, King Solomon announces that, as he is growing old and infirm, both he and Hiram, King of Tyre, have agreed to select Levi to succeed King Solomon as Right Worshipful Master of the Temple-Lodge upon the death of Solomon, and to this end, they intend to induct Levi into the Oriental Chair. After the kings have done this, Solomon, King of Israel orders the Officers to return to their Stations and Places. Levi takes the South; King Solomon returning to his Station in the East, falters as he attempts to step up to his place. He is aided to that Station by one of the East Gate guards. Solomon then instructs the Craft in the use of the Grip of Past Master, aided by the East Gate guard. He instructs the Lodge in the proper use of the Constitution, By-Laws, care of the records and use of the Gavel. The Crown is placed upon the head of Levi, and the three Council Officers go arm-in-arm out of the Chamber. When they are gone, the regular Officers of the Lodge replace the guards by taking their own Stations and Places, after which the work of the Degree is taken up with the Candidate at the altar, where the square, etc., are emblematically presented to him.

King Solomon enters wearing his robes. His crown rests on a stand in the East. He is seated in front of the Secretary's desk on the main floor. Note: SGG = South Gate Guard; WGG = West Gate Guard; EGG = East Gate Guard).

SGG   *(As King Solomon enters)* The King! The King!

WGG   *(As King Solomon passes West Gate)* Live forever, O King!

EGG   *(As King passes East Gate)* Hail, Most Excellent King Solomon!

Hiram King of Tyre now enters and proceeds to the East by way of the South).

SGG   Who comes here? Who approaches at the South Gate?

HKT   Hiram, King of Tyre, the friend of Solomon.

SGG   *(Stands aside)* Hiram, King of Tyre has ever the permission to enter. Pass on.

Hiram King of Tyre now proceeds to the West.

WGG   Who comes here? Who approaches at the South Gate?

HKT   Hiram, King of Tyre, the friend of Solomon.

WGG   *(Stands aside)* Hiram, King of Tyre has ever the permission to enter. Pass on.

Hiram King of Tyre now proceeds to the East.

EGG   Who comes here? Who approaches the Throne of the Mighty King?

HKT Hiram, King of Tyre, the friend of Solomon.

WGG *(Addressing King Solomon)* O Mighty King Solomon, Hiram, King of Tyre is approaching.

KS Hiram, my friend, a thousand thanks for your attendance here at my request.

HKT Most Excellent King Solomon, your joy at this meeting is equaled by my own. The ends of the earth would not be outside the length of my cable-tow when summoned by you to a Lodge over which you so ably preside.

KS Many years have passed and much has happened since you and I wrought together, and I have in the course of nature but a short time left in which to plan for the future, and as we three did agree, in the past, so I trust you and I can arrive at a wise decision. Sit down and let me spread my thoughts before you.

Kings now pantomime a deep discussion in low tone. Levi, a Workman, enters and approaches the South Gate.

SGG *(Stopping Levi with upraised hand)* Who comes here? Who seeks to enter the presence of the Great Kings?

Levi A Craftsman of the Temple seeks audience with King Solomon.

SGG Return, Craftsman. None are permitted to enter the Temple at this irregular hour. Whence came you?

Levi From a Lodge of the Holy Saints John of Jerusalem.

SGG Then you are a Mason, I presume.

Levi I am so taken and accepted among Brethren and Fellows.

SGG Give me the password of Entered Apprentice *(Done)*. Pass on.

WGG Who approaches the West Gate? Are you a Fellowcraft?

Levi I am, try me.

WGG By what will you be tried?

Levi By the square.

WGG Why by the square?

Levi Because it is an emblem of morality and one of the Working Tools of Fellowcraft.

WGG Give me the password of Fellowcraft *(Done)*. Pass on.

EGG *(Meeting Levi part way to the East Gate)* Who comes here?

Levi   A Craftsman, come by order of Solomon the Wise.

EGG   Are you a Master Mason?

Levi   I am.

EGG   What makes you a Master Mason?

Levi   My Obligation.

EGG   Give me the password of Master Mason *(Done)*. The pass is right, but we have no orders to admit anyone at this late hour. You will have to turn back.

Levi   *(Turning slowly and going towards the West, raises his hands as if about to give the Grand Hailing Sign of Master Mason, and realizing that it cannot be seen in darkness, drops his hands and exclaims)* OMGWTNTHTWS? *(The East Guard, hearing these words, calls out to Levi).*

EGG   Brother Levi, advance to the East Gate; and I shall seek to admit you. *(Speaking to King Solomon)* O Mighty King Solomon, a Craftsman seeks to enter. He claims it is in answer to your order.

KS   It is well. Admit him. *(Speaking to HKT)* This should be the Craftsman of whom I have been speaking.

HKT   Let us examine him and prove that he is the proper man.

KS   *(To Levi)* Brother Levi, communicate to me the substitute for the Master's Word.

Levi   Place yourself in the proper position to receive it, and I will.

KS   What is the proper position?

Levi   X   *(Done)*.

KS   I am satisfied *(Kings are seated. Levi salaams before the Kings)*. Hiram, King of Tyre, Levi is here by my summons. It was he who found the body of our Grand Master Hiram Abif. *(To Levi)* Brother Levi, your ardent labors have long merited recognition. Hiram, King of Tyre and myself have agreed that, as you have labored, so shall you be rewarded. Inasmuch as life and death are for me constant companions, it has been agreed that upon my death, you, Levi, have been chosen to take my place and preside over the Lodge.

Levi   O Mighty King, Live Forever *(Falls on his knees as he speaks)*.

KS   Yes, Brother Levi, the time of my departure is near. But you shall have your reward.

Levi   O King, shall I now receive the true word?

KS No, that will come later. Only the wisdom of future generations shall determine or bring to light the True Word. Brother Hiram, King of Tyre, assist me in the task of installing Brother Levi in my place, in preparation for the possibility of my death.

Levi *(Falling face to the floor, crying)* I am unworthy to sit in the oriental Chair of the Grand Master.

KS *(Assisting Levi to his feet)* Rise, my Brother. You say that you are unworthy! Do you not remember the one great prerequisite to the occupying of the Master's Chair? "Of who best can work and best agree"?

(King Solomon and King Hiram then install Levi as Master in the Chair).

*** Brethren, this my Station in the East of all Lodges, shall be hereafter known as the Oriental Chair, in remembrance of me and in token of Brotherly love. Let each of you in the future, when assuming this Station, be installed therein by two or more faithful Past Masters, aiding you by this grip *(exchanges the Grip of Past Master with Levi in the sight of all)* and by investing each with the name of the same. And as I have worn the Crown, so each Installed Master shall be covered, while the rest of the Brethren remain uncovered. And as I have ruled you with the use of a Gavel, so shall each succeeding Master rule the Brethren *(places crown on Levi and extends him the gavel)*. I now declare the Station of Master is filled. *.

Seats the Brethren, then the three, King Solomon, Hiram King of Tyre and Levi walk out of the room. When these Officers have left, followed by the Guards, the regular Officers resume their Station and Places. The work is taken up again where it had been suspended, which was at that place where the Candidate had received the Grip and Word.

CPSIA information can be obtained
at www.ICGtesting.com
Printed in the USA
BVHW010138090120
568988BV00014B/164/P